JINNY YU

Goose Lane Editions

AT ONCE

À LA FOIS

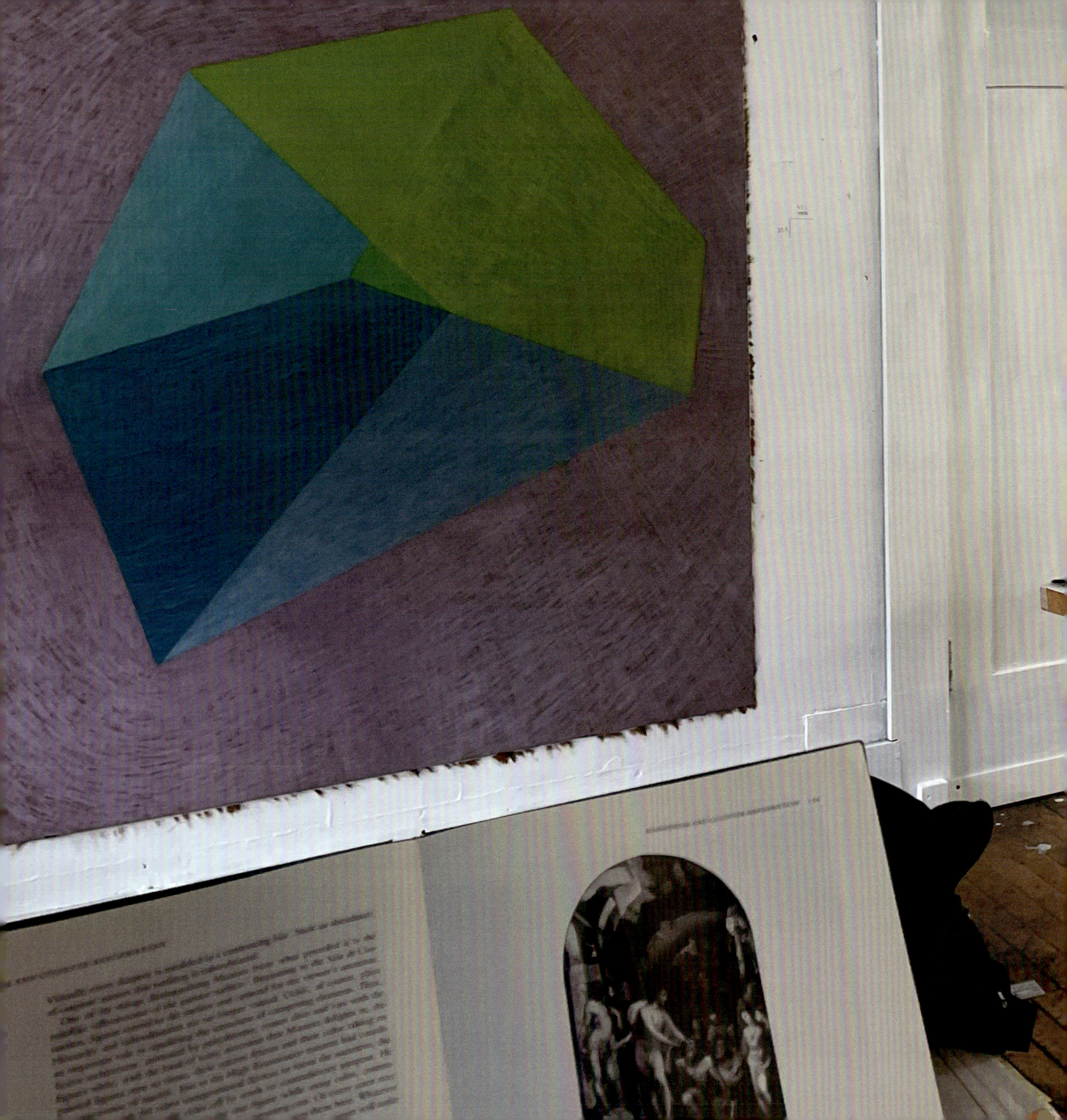

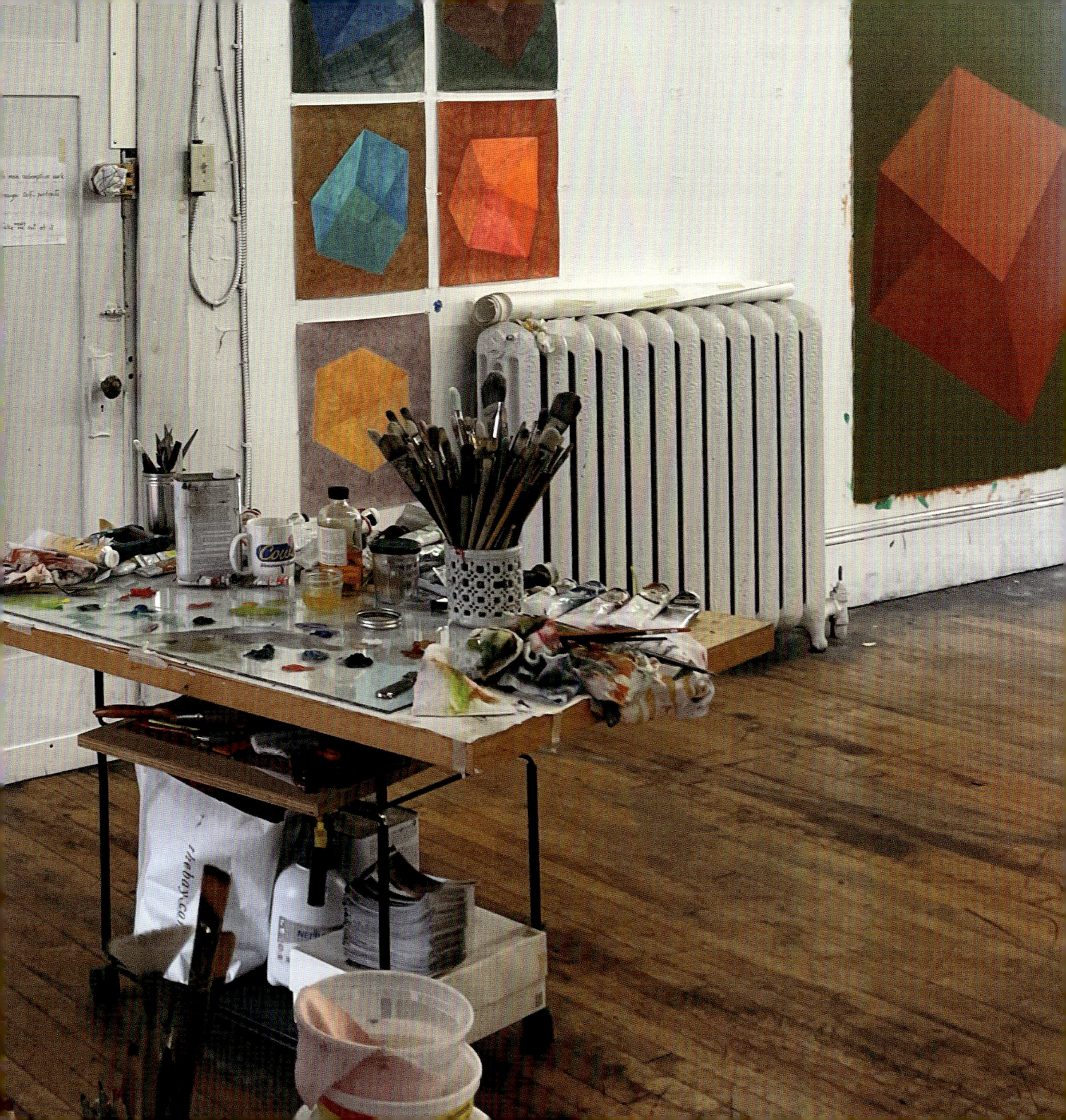

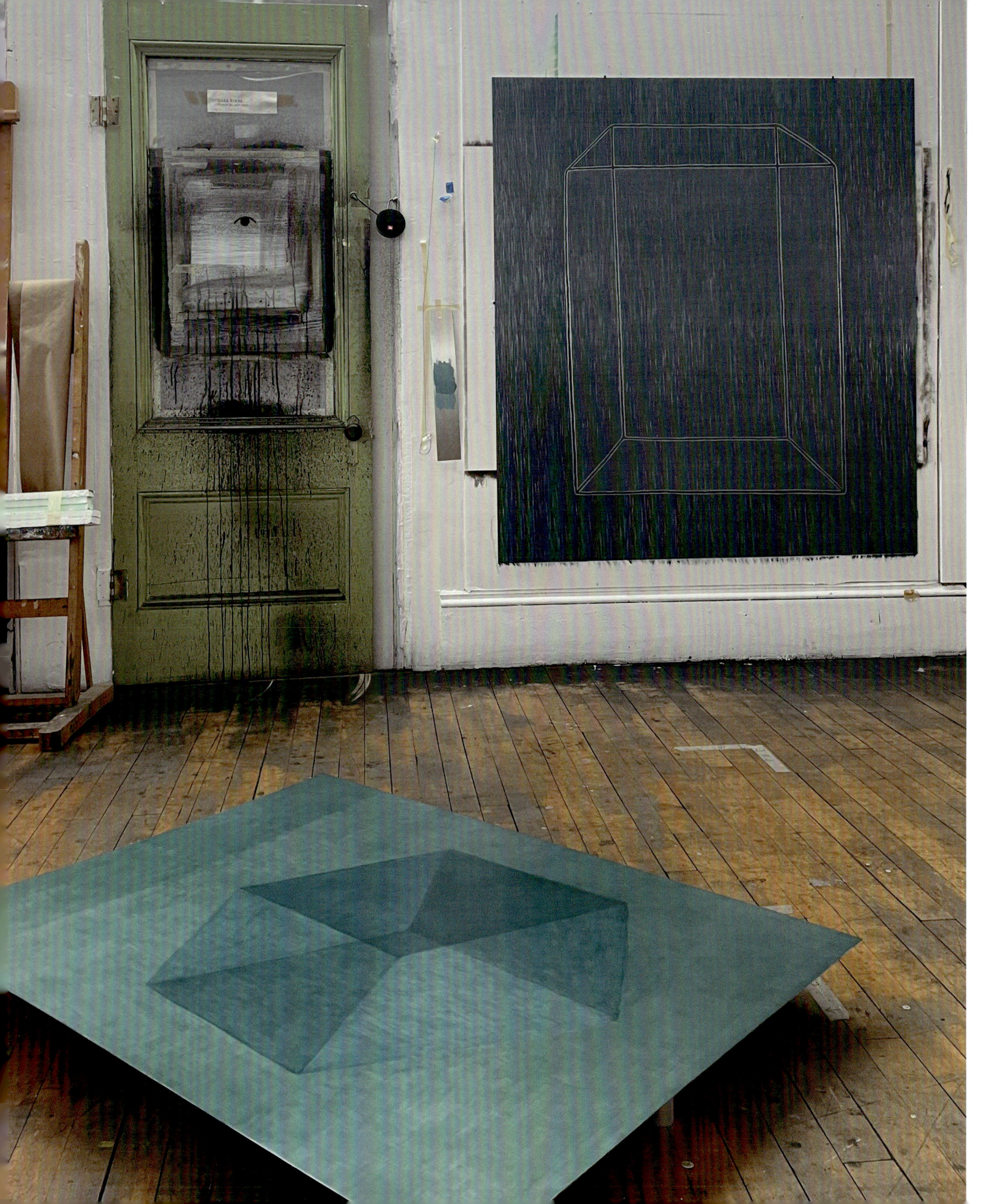

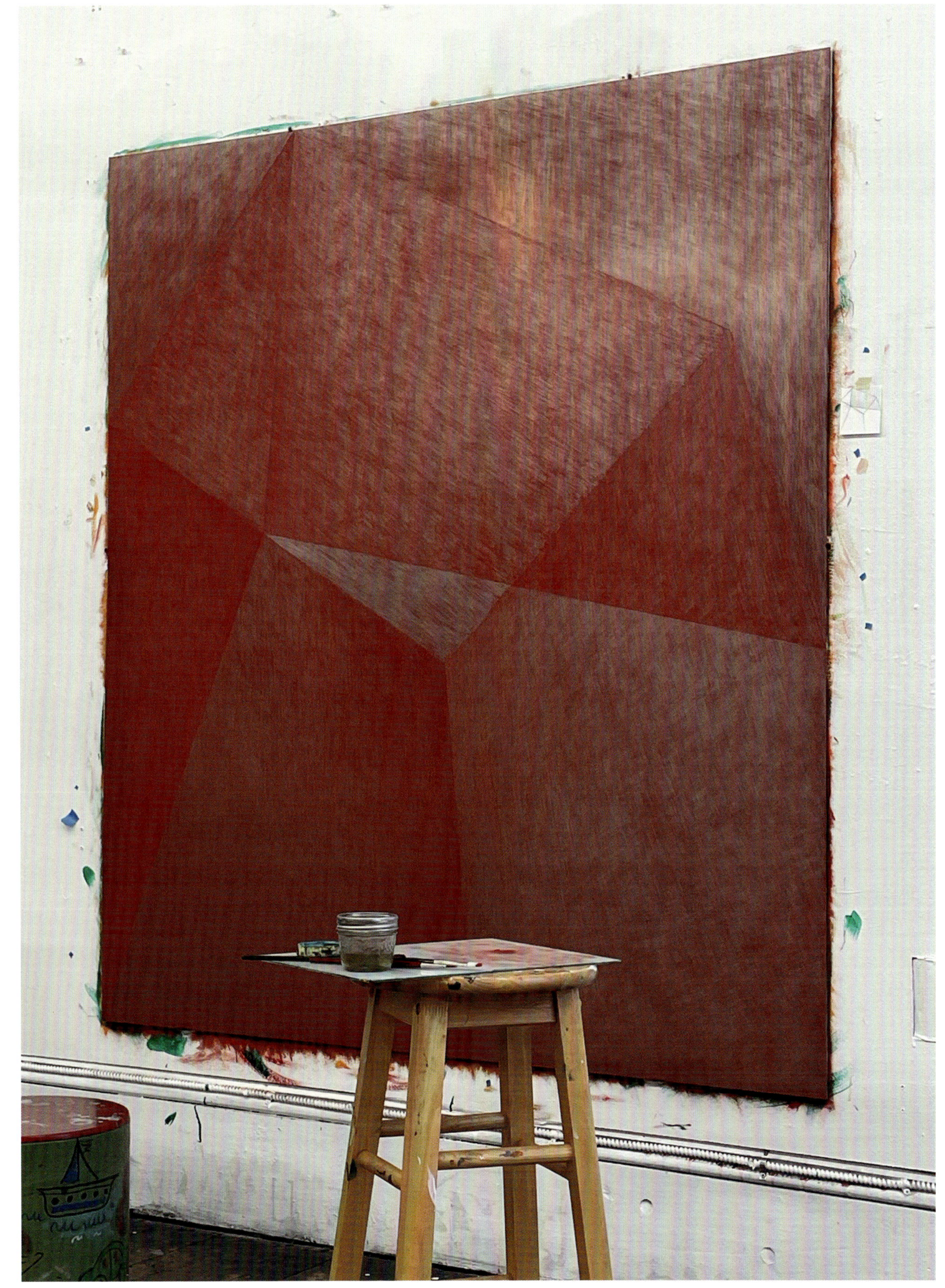

Three complementary perspectives and sensibilities are brought together in this monographic publication devoted to the latest work of the artist Jinny Yu, a brilliant painter, professor, and activist whose practice continues to enrich the contemporary history of abstraction in painting. In tune with the societal and political realities of the world in which she lives, she adopts formally abstract language to reflect on her experience of migration and nomadism in a socially engaged manner. Always interacting with space and place, the artist takes inspiration from three-dimensional territory drawn between Seoul, where she was born; Ottawa, where she teaches; Montréal and Toronto, where she was trained; Venice and New York, where she has lived; Berlin, where she regularly sojourns; and the many other cities that have welcomed her in residence over the years.

In their contributions to this book, Patrick Flores, Professor of Art Studies at the University of the Philippines and Deputy Director at National Gallery Singapore, Ming Tiampo, Professor of Art History and co-director of the Centre for Transnational Cultural Analysis at Carleton University, and Georgiana Uhlyarik, Curator, Canadian Art and co-lead of the Indigenous + Canadian Art Department at the Art Gallery of Ontario (AGO), chronicle the various issues Jinny Yu has interwoven in her painting practice, from the exhibition *Don't They Ever Stop Migrating?* (2015), presented during the 56th Venice Biennale, to her recent works exhibited at the AGO (2024). The authors also examine Yu's community and networks, in particular her associations with artist Lani Maestro, whom she met while studying at Concordia University, and the research group Canadian BIPOC Artists Rolodex, which she founded and directs with three team members and nineteen advisory committee members with a view to creating an inventory of Canadian artists who are Black, Indigenous, and People of Colour, to further the visibility, teaching, and dissemination of their work.

This monograph is conceived as a counterpoint to an eponymous exhibition presented in 2024 at the AGO. In 2025, the exhibition will be hosted by the Guido Molinari Foundation, which the artist visited while studying with Molinari at Concordia University. The presentation of Yu's work in this space, once the studio of one of the most influential practitioners of geometric abstraction, is a significant moment. For over ten years, the foundation Molinari created has welcomed artists whose practice is marked by historical awareness, and curators who engage in dialogues between generations of artists. Although Yu's career is rooted in a historical affiliation that resonates with the abstraction that Molinari and his contemporaries developed, her work provides striking points of difference that are of particular interest.

Paint is a material that enables us to grasp the world and reconsider the way we perceive it and respond to it. What Molinari called *l'espace réversible* (reversible space), a Quebec variation on the American "push and pull," is something that Yu views as a dialogue between host and guest. Though the foundations in abstraction differ, they both display an articulate capacity to energize the surface of their work by way of chromatic contrasts. For Molinari's former student, colour is not reduced to a pure wave frequency, whose vibratory effect emerges at the edge of the colour planes. The endowment of space with an expressive value and a critical dimension is a facet that has recently reappeared in Yu's work. Her painting is a gateway through which colour charts a conceptual path between chromatic space, cultural identity, and societal issues.

As an immigrant from Seoul and a settler in Ottawa on the unceded territory of the Anishinabe Algonquin Nation, Jinny Yu has spent the last few years creating a body of drawings titled *Hôte* (host and/or guest), whose autobiographical underpinnings take root in the ambiguity inherent in the French term. How can one reconcile the colonial nature of history with the notion of hospitality? How do you develop a sense of belonging and kinship with a community, and establish a home on an unceded territory, in a responsible manner? These questions are at the core of Yu's artistic practice, which offers an astute vehicle to think about the history of abstraction and the representational regimes that shape our understanding of history.

Jinny Yu's works are at once fluid and structured, in motion and always formally embodied. A language shaped by experience and bodily memory becomes *Inextricably Ours*. Painting, abstraction, identity, and representation converse across the walls of her exhibitions, structuring spaces of resonance between images, places, homes, territories, and societies.

Marie-Eve Beaupré
General and artistic director
Guido Molinari Foundation

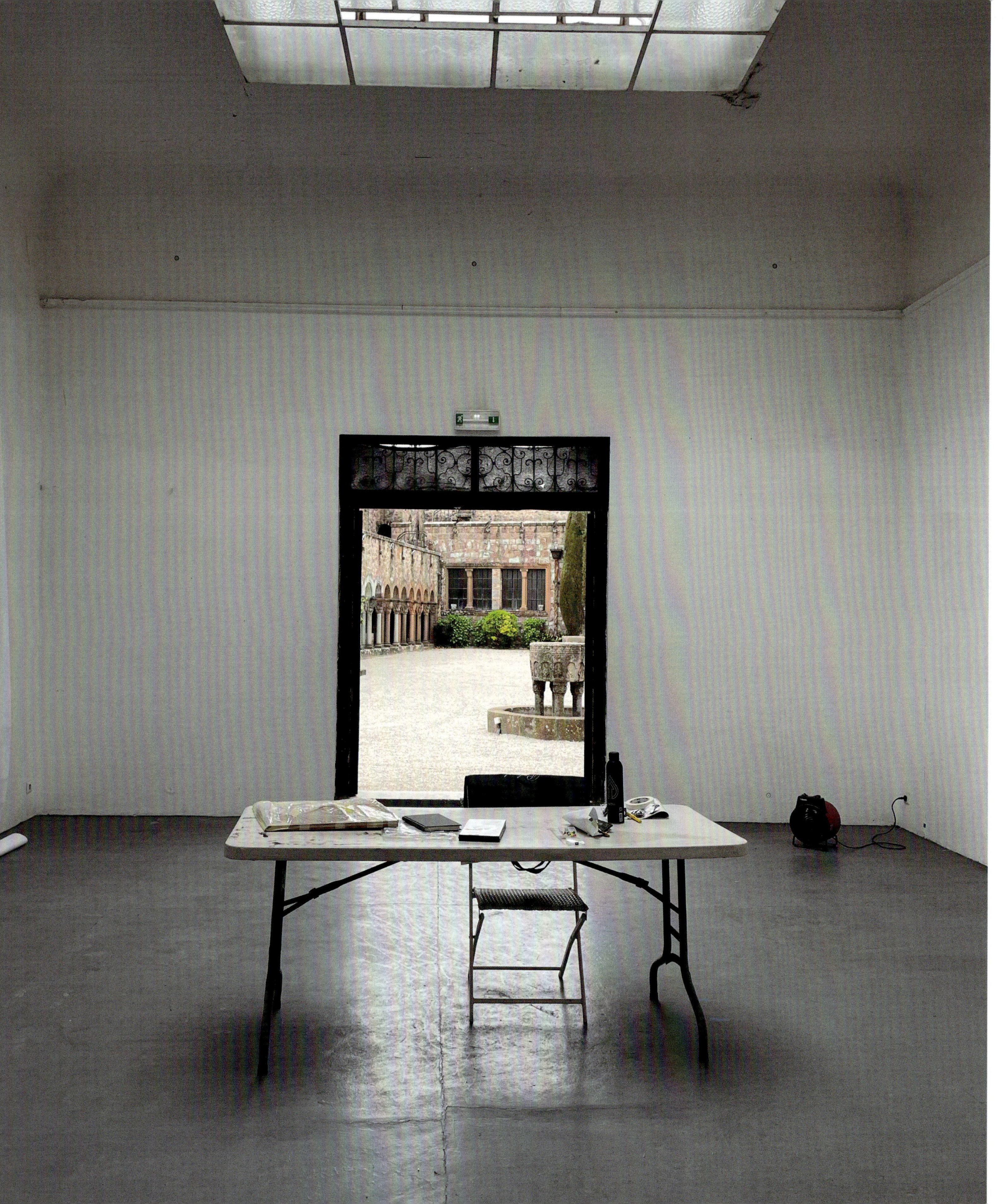

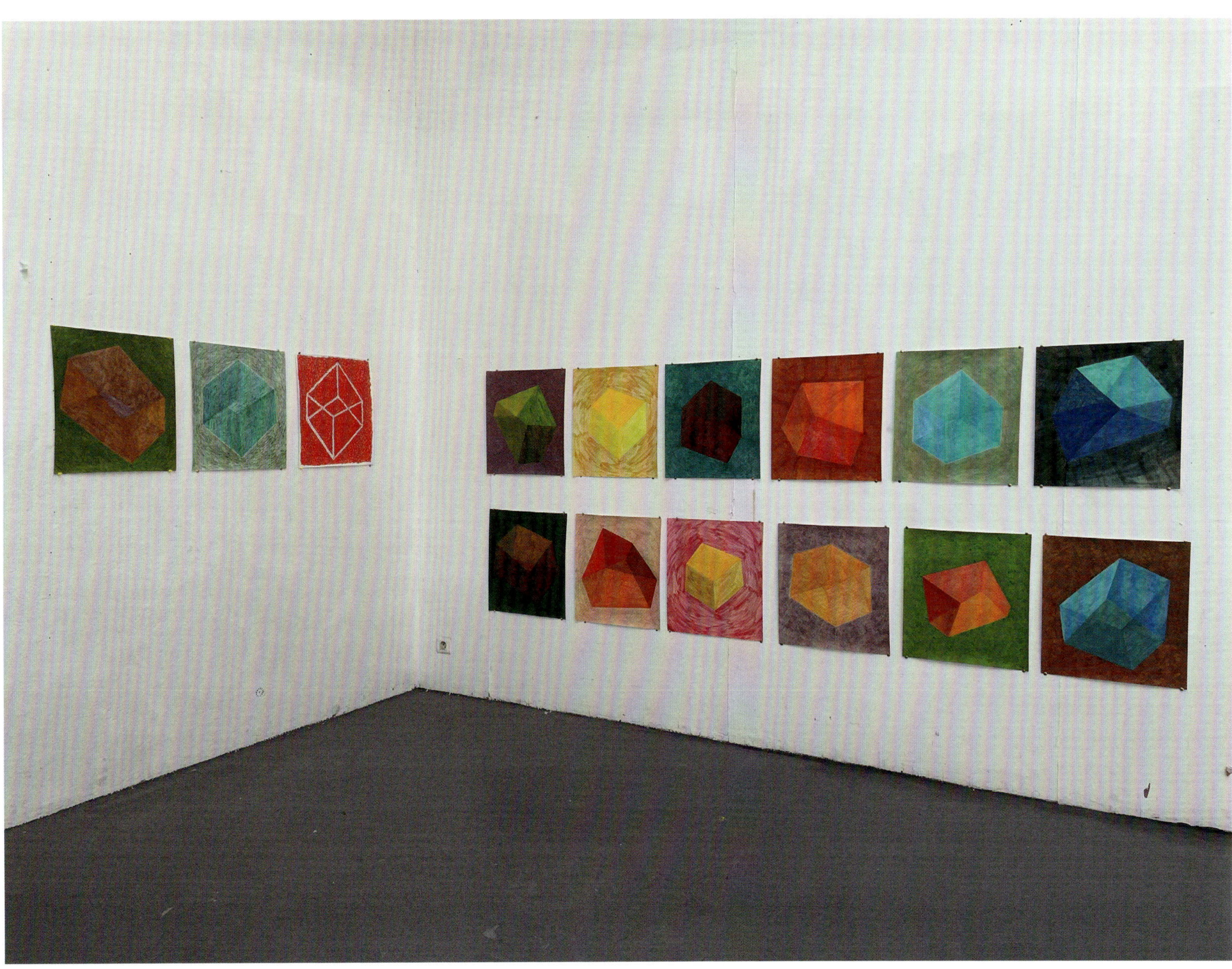

Trois regards et sensibilités complémentaires sont réunis dans cette publication monographique consacrée au plus récent travail de l'artiste Jinny Yu, une brillante peintre, professeure et activiste dont la pratique enrichit l'histoire contemporaine de l'abstraction en peinture. Perméable aux réalités sociales et politiques du monde dans lequel elle évolue, elle adopte un langage formellement abstrait qui s'avère socialement engagé dans une réflexion sur l'expérience de la migration et de la nomadicité. Constamment en interaction avec l'espace et le lieu où elle travaille, l'artiste s'inspire du territoire tridimensionnel déployé entre Séoul, où elle est née, Ottawa, où elle enseigne, Montréal et Toronto, où elle a été formée, Venise et New York, où elle a vécu, Berlin, où elle séjourne régulièrement, ainsi que les nombreuses autres villes qui l'ont accueillie en résidence au fil des années.

Patrick Flores, professeur en études des arts à l'Université des Philippines et directeur adjoint de la National Gallery Singapore, Ming Tiampo, professeure en histoire de l'art et codirectrice du Centre for Transnational Cultural Analysis à l'Université Carleton, et Georgiana Uhlyarik, conservatrice et codirectrice du Département d'art autochtone et canadien au Musée des beaux-arts de l'Ontario (MBAO), témoignent dans cet ouvrage des divers enjeux entrelacés dans la peinture de Jinny Yu depuis l'exposition *Don't They Ever Stop Migrating?* (2015), présentée pendant la 56e Biennale de Venise, jusqu'aux œuvres récentes exposées au MBAO (2024). L'écosystème de ses affinités est également abordé, notamment sa complicité avec Lani Maestro, rencontrée lors de ses études à l'Université Concordia, et le groupe de recherche Canadian BIPOC Artists Rolodex, qu'elle a fondé et qu'elle dirige avec trois membres d'équipe et 19 membres d'un comité consultatif en vue de créer un inventaire des artistes autochtones, noirs et de couleur au Canada pour accroître le rayonnement, l'enseignement et la diffusion de leur travail.

Cette monographie est conçue en contrepoint d'une exposition éponyme présentée en 2024 au MBAO. En 2025, les œuvres de Jinny Yu seront accueillies par la Fondation Guido Molinari, lieu fréquenté par l'artiste alors qu'elle étudiait à l'Université Concordia auprès de Molinari. Il s'avère hautement significatif de présenter les œuvres de Jinny Yu dans ce lieu qui fut autrefois l'atelier d'un des plus influents praticiens de l'abstraction géométrique. Depuis plus de dix ans, la Fondation qu'il a créée accueille des artistes dont la pratique est dotée d'une conscience historique et des commissaires qui désirent engager des dialogues entre les générations de praticiens. Bien que le parcours de Jinny Yu s'inscrive dans une filiation historique en résonance avec l'abstraction développée par Molinari et ses contemporains, il offre de fertiles points de dissonance qui nous intéresseront particulièrement.

La peinture est un matériau qui permet de saisir le monde et de reconsidérer la manière dont nous le percevons et résonnons avec lui. Ce que Molinari nommait l'espace réversible, une variation québécoise du «push and pull» américain, Jinny Yu l'envisage en tant que dialogue entre hôte (*host*) et hôte (*guest*). Leurs ancrages dans l'abstraction diffèrent, mais ils possèdent tous deux cette éloquente capacité à dynamiser la surface de leurs œuvres au moyen de contrastes chromatiques. Pour celle qui fut un jour l'élève, la couleur ne se réduit pas à une pure fréquence ondulatoire, dont l'effet de vibration se situe à la frontière des pans colorés. Récemment réapparue dans son travail, elle munit l'espace d'une valeur expressive et d'une dimension critique. Sa peinture est un portail par lequel la couleur trace une voie conceptuelle entre l'espace chromatique, l'identité culturelle et les enjeux sociétaux.

Au cours des dernières années, Jinny Yu a réalisé, en tant qu'immigrante de Séoul actuellement établie (*settler*) à Ottawa sur le territoire non cédé de la Nation Anishinabe Algonquine, un corpus de dessins intitulé *Hôte* dont les assises autobiographiques puisent leurs sources dans l'ambiguïté du terme en français. Comment concilier la nature coloniale de l'histoire et la notion d'hospitalité? Comment développer un sentiment d'appartenance et de filiation avec une communauté et établir avec bienveillance sa demeure sur un territoire non cédé? Ces questions sociétales se logent au cœur de la réflexion picturale de l'artiste, un judicieux véhicule pour réfléchir à l'histoire de l'abstraction et aux régimes de représentation qui marquent notre compréhension de l'histoire.

Les œuvres de Jinny Yu sont à la fois fluides et structurées, en mouvement et toujours formellement incarnées. Lorsque façonné par l'expérience et la mémoire du corps, un langage devient *Inextricablement Nôtre*. Peinture, abstraction, identité et représentation conversent sur les cimaises de ses expositions, structurant des espaces de résonance entre des images, des lieux, des demeures, des territoires et des sociétés.

Marie-Eve Beaupré
Directrice générale et artistique
Fondation Guido Molinari

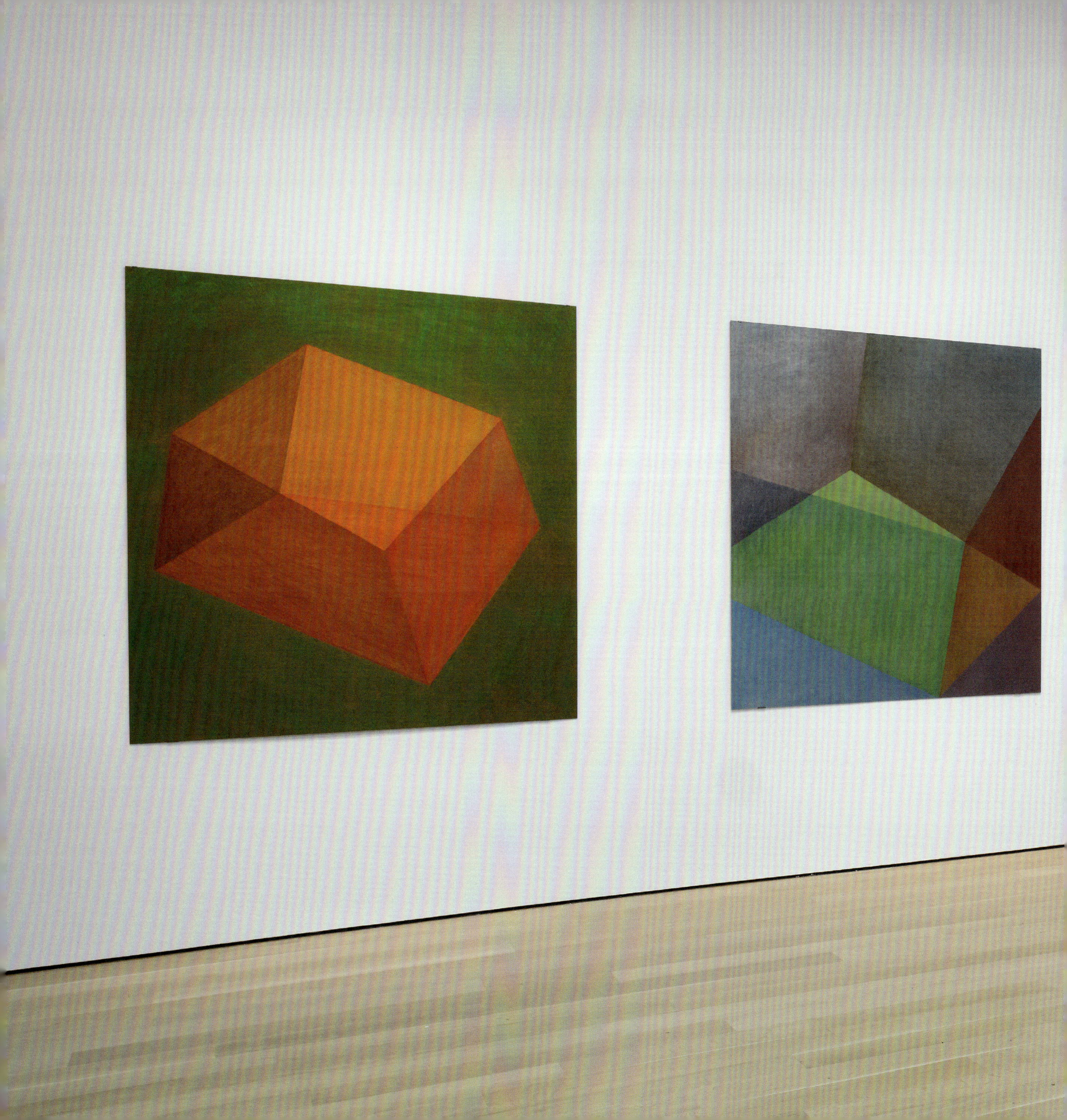

Jinny Yu is in Between + All at Once

Georgiana Uhlyarik

Jinny Yu est entre les deux et tout à la fois

Georgiana Uhlyarik

Installation view | vue d'installation
JINNY YU: AT ONCE
June 22, 2024 – January 5, 2025 |
22 juin 2024 – 5 janvier 2025
Art Gallery of Ontario | Musée
des beaux-arts de l'Ontario, Toronto

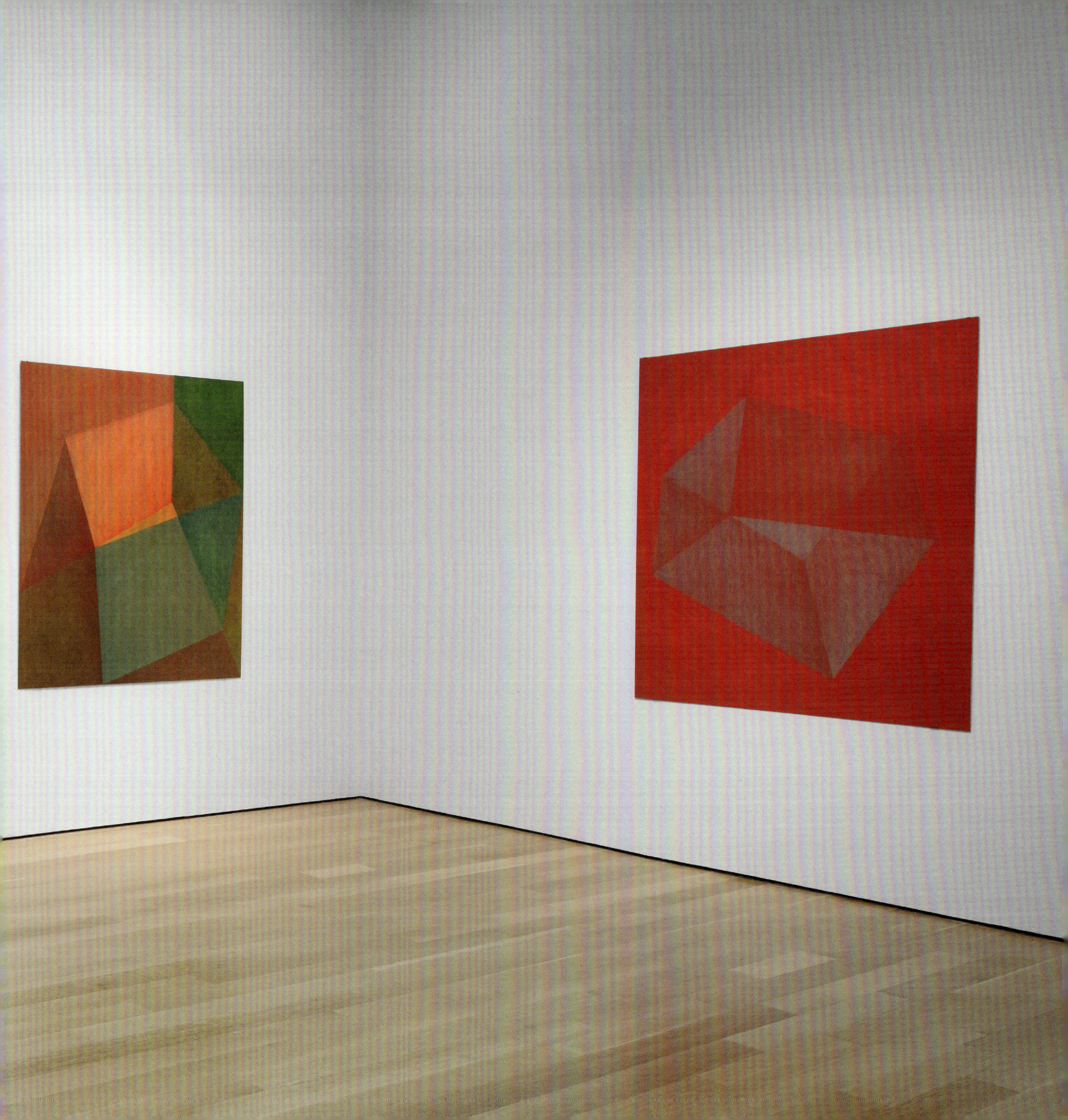

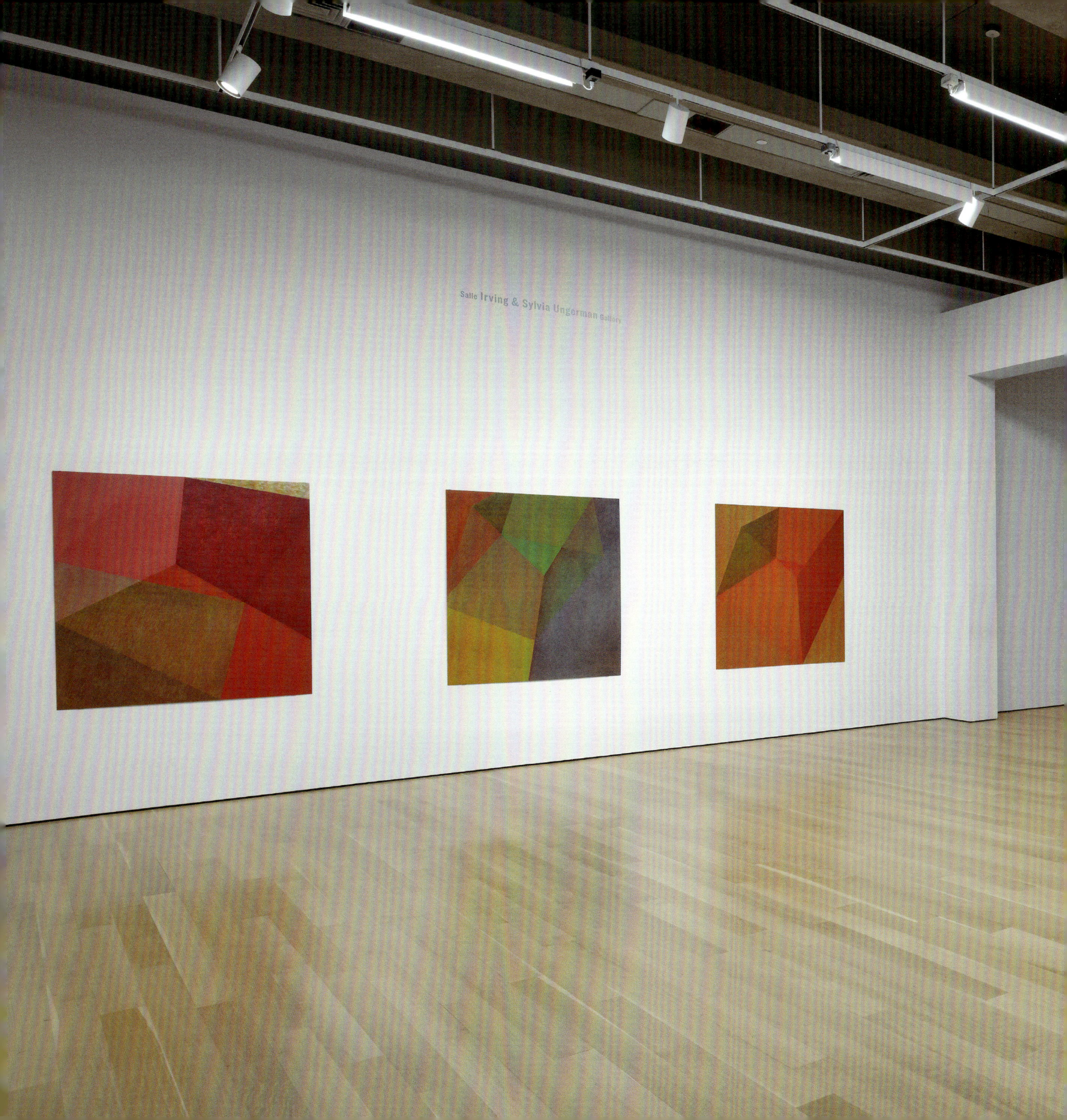
Salle Irving & Sylvia Ungerman Gallery

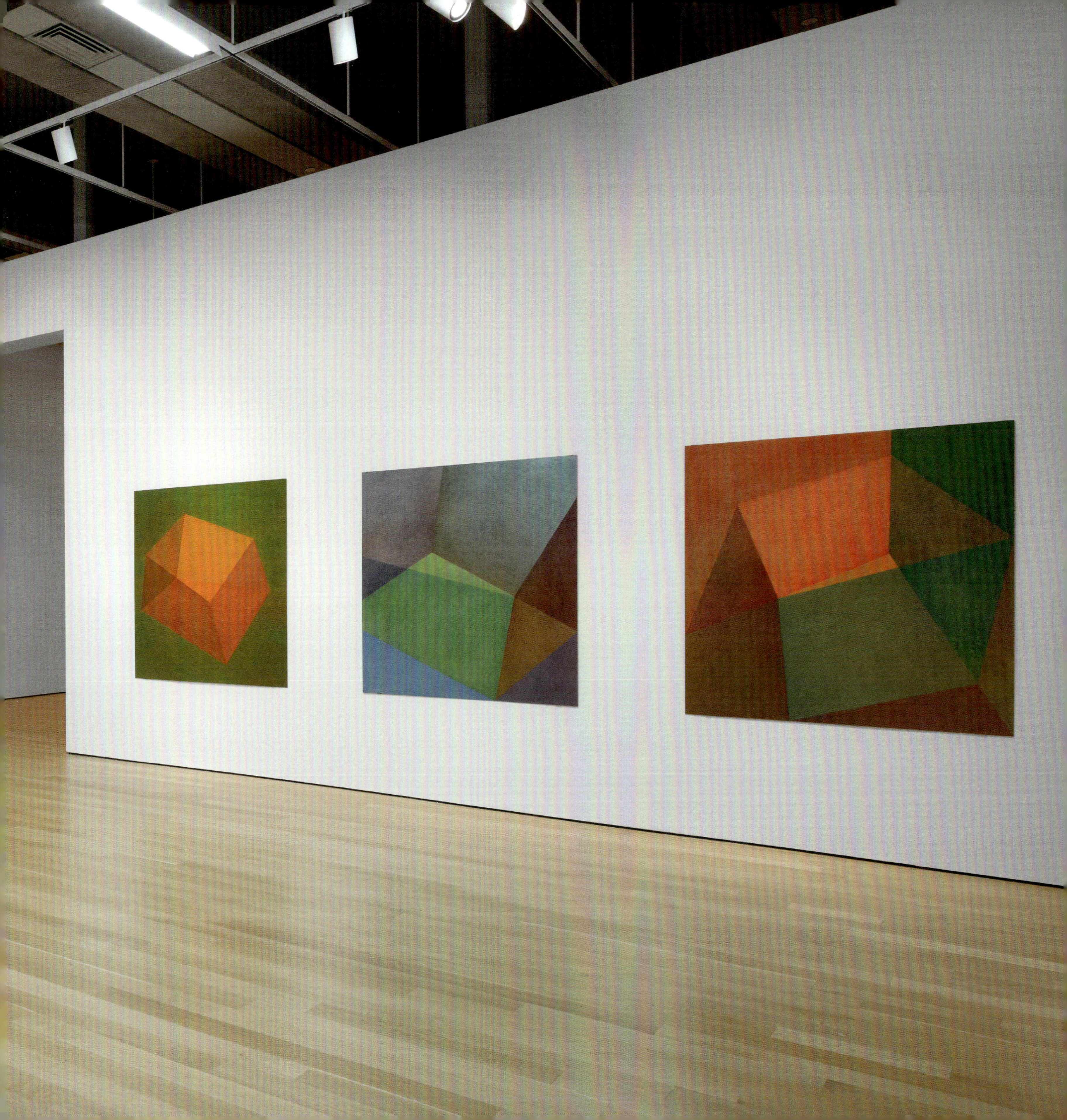

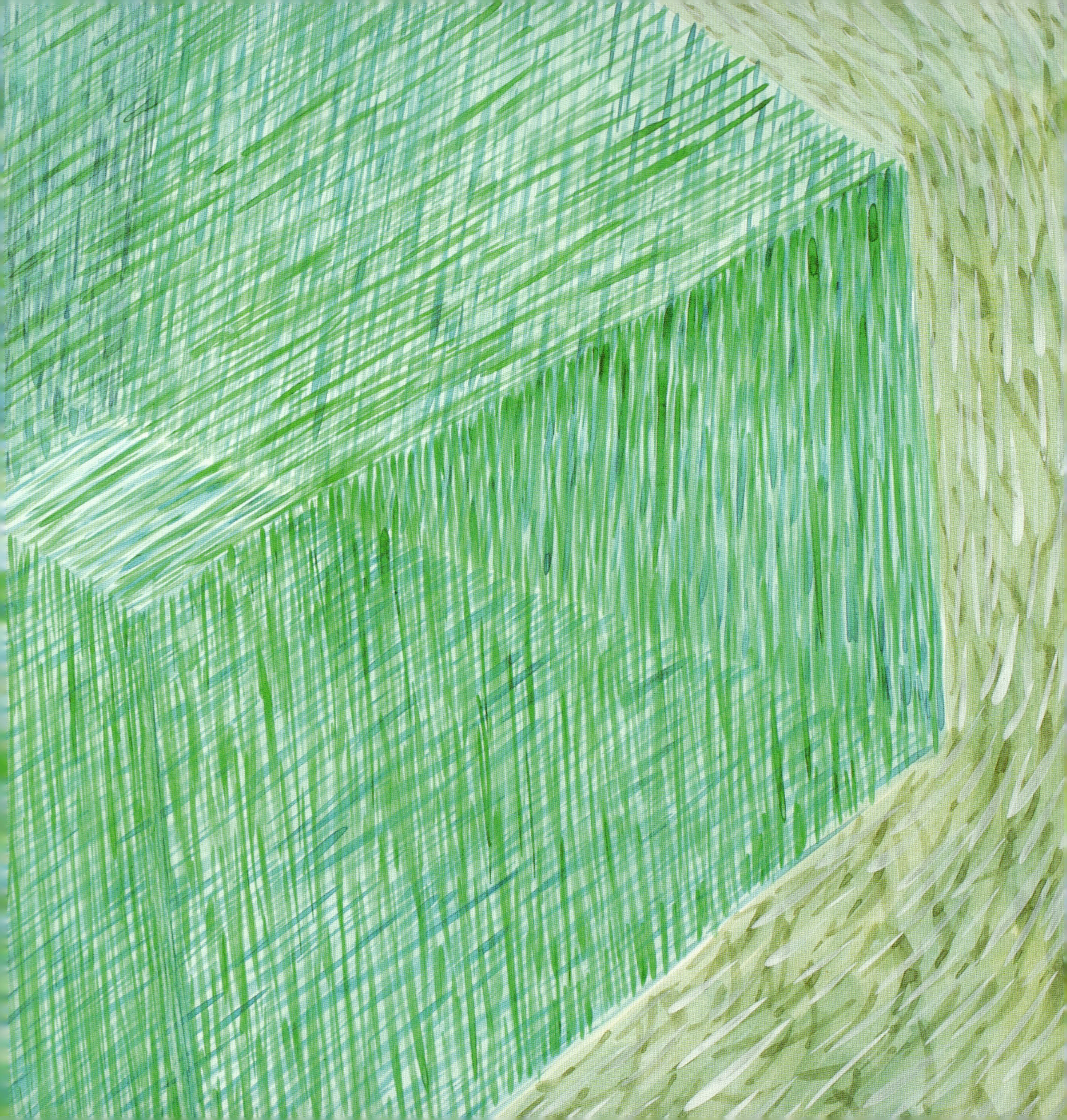

I am writing during the three days of Chuseok — the Korean autumn harvest festival — and only days after the 2023 autumnal equinox, when light and dark split the day in half around the planet. It is a time when the sun appears directly above the earth's equator, bringing the two hemispheres in equal balance as they begin their forthcoming journey, extending their reach into the other's day or night. It is also the third time Canada has marked the National Day for Truth and Reconciliation, observed on September 30 of each year since 2021 — a day of remembrance of and reflection on the violent and unjust history of colonialism in these territories, and our shared responsibility to seek truth and justice for Indigenous peoples and honour their sovereignty.

At the gathering of these seemingly unrelated yet entangled occasions, Jinny Yu's new colourful and kaleidoscopic paintings and works on paper could be contextualized. In recent years, Yu has awakened new research interests, realizing new complexities regarding notions of belonging to a place, a state of statelessness and acceptance of displacement as a human condition. The nuance of "not having a place to belong to at all, instead of not being able to belong"[1] may be slight but is a critical difference in shifting understanding of the possibility of connectedness and the imposing weight of historical events.

Inextricably Ours W22-06 (detail | détail), 2022
watercolour on paper | aquarelle sur papier
48 × 44 cm

The works in her new series, *Inextricably Ours*, represent a journey of nearly three years of research, painting, and several artist residencies as she questioned

* *As always, I would like to thank Ihor Holubizky for everlasting and winding conversations about art, artists, and the creative act, among many, many other things.*

1 Unless otherwise noted, all artist quotes are from discussion with the artist, August 14, 2023 in her Ottawa studio.

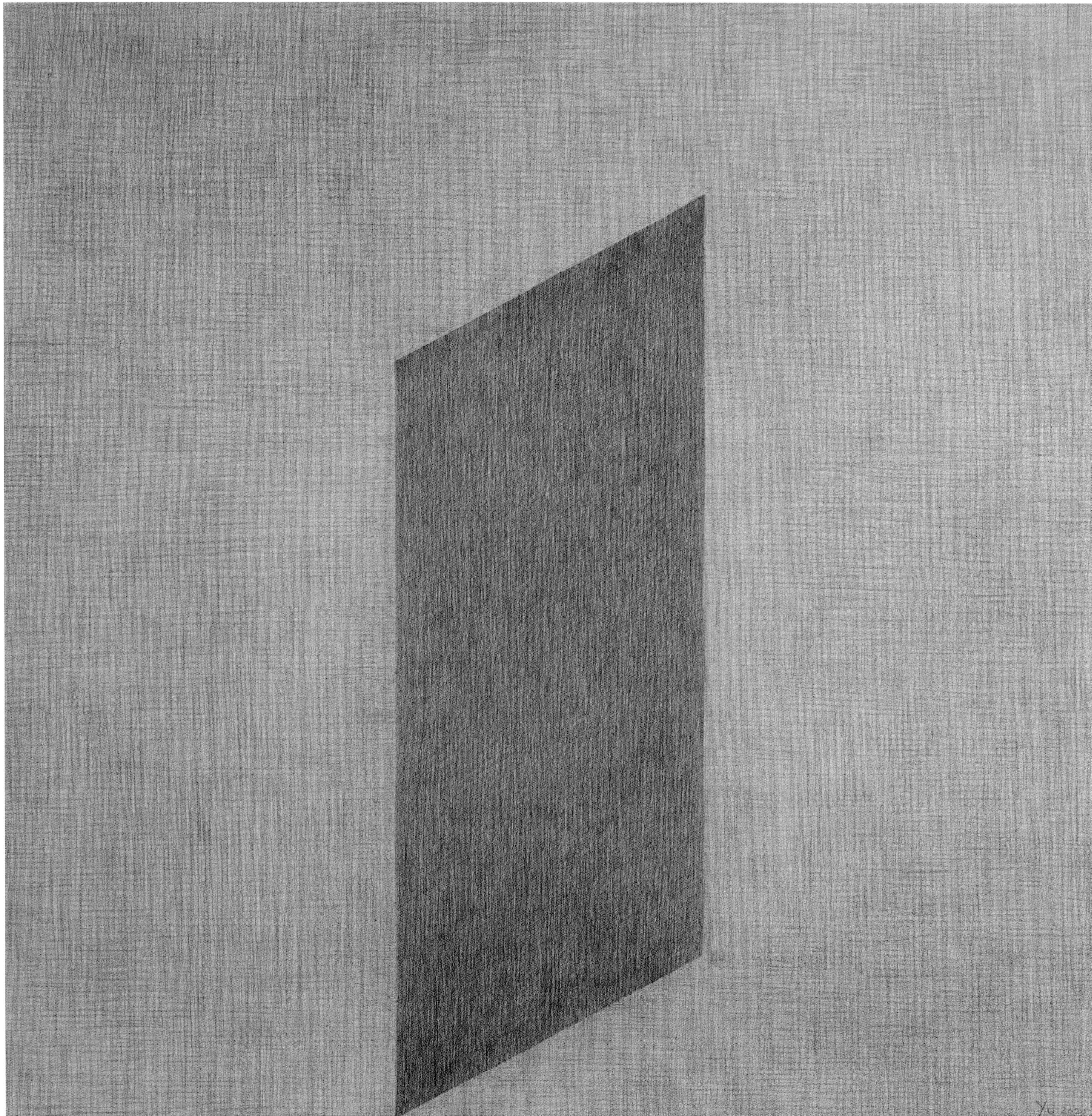

and re-examined the "binary of hosthood and guesthood," re-tuning her pictorial language of abstraction.[2] As Yu says, after *Perpetual Guest* (2019) — her installation of painting on glass — and *Hôte* (2020) — her drawings and artist book — she wanted to linger longer on the troubled guest/host relationship, and challenge the limitations of these established positions.

Yu set out to make paintings that take time, that are laborious, careful, and open-ended, not knowing where they might lead. Her work had dwelled during the past 14 years in a conceptual realm where she was "questioning what painting is, beyond the image."[3] Painting had been a verb for her — an action that constitutes a painting, a gesture, mechanical brushwork. A series of unsettling artistic questions coupled with disturbing social global events and deep personal reflection necessitated Yu's reconsideration of the undeniably generative role of the image in painting. A shape emerged in her drawings and with it her inescapable "problem of background," as she calls it. Not long after — perhaps inevitably — her work welcomed once again, and with full force, a release of colour.

Hôte XL, 2020
graphite on paper | graphite sur papier
42 × 42 cm
Private collection | collection privée

Yu's three-year journey began slowly and sensitively in late 2020. She was striving to process the ongoing COVID-19 pandemic and its amplification of anti-Asian racism, and the mounting civil unrest condemning systemic racial discrimination. Earlier that year, she had produced and exhibited *Hôte*, 42 graphite drawings — a set that resulted from a daily practiced task — that she made into an artist book.[4] Meant to be experienced sequentially, it begins with a tall, dark rectangle placed centrally on a blank square. The figure/ground relationship suggests the guest/host positionality. The combination of three words guided her thinking: "Can guest host? Can host guest? Guest can host. Host can guest."[5] With each new drawing, the relationship between drawn space and the white of the sheet is reconstituted. Over the series, light and dark grey hatching emerges into grey-on-grey compositions and eventually takes over the full page, blurring positionality and opening up possibilities. Further on, the rectangle is placed at

2 Artist statement for *JINNY YU: AT ONCE* at the Art Gallery of Ontario, Toronto (June 22, 2024 – January 5, 2025).

3 Jinny Yu, quoted in *Jinny Yu: to activate space* (Montréal, Québec: Éditions Art Mûr, 2014), 43.

4 For more on *Hôte* see "Hôte," Art Mûr, accessed November 25, 2023, https://artmur.com/en/artists/jinny-yu/hote and view video walk-through of artist book *HÔTE* (2021), Korean Cultural Centre Canada, "Virtual Artist Studio Visit: Jinny Yu," March 25, 2021, YouTube Video, 5:00, https://www.youtube.com/watch?v=4n33OcjDCls. Hôte is now part of the Montreal Museum of Fine Arts Collection.

5 "Virtual Artist Studio Visit"

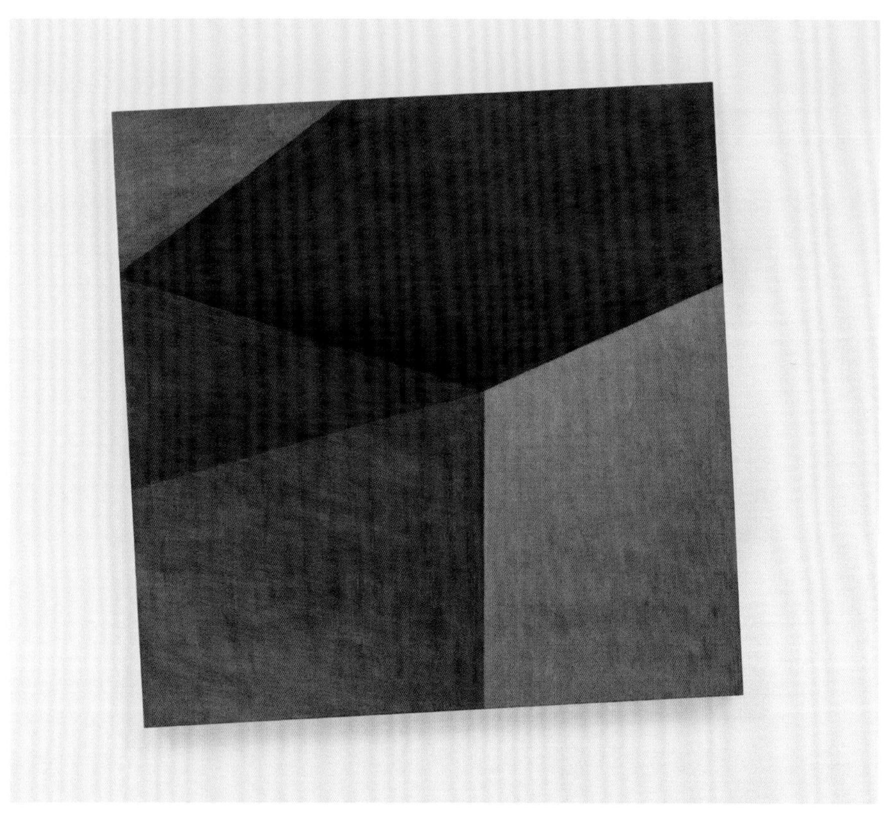

why does its lock fit my key?, 2018
oil on aluminium | huile sur aluminium
66 × 66 cm

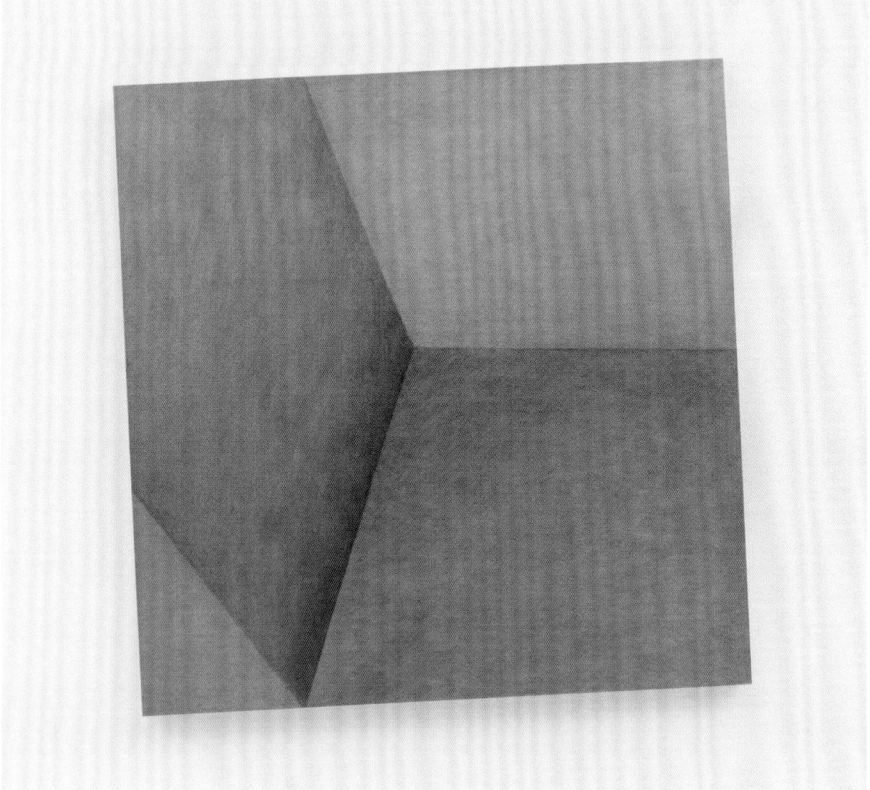

why does its lock fit my key?, 2018
oil on aluminium | huile sur aluminium
66 × 66 cm

an acute angle — perhaps a door slightly ajar — evoking a third dimension. It concludes with the sheet covered in graphite hatching, at the centre of which is a very narrow, vertical space left bare save one thin line in the centre.P. 46

In its formal simplicity, the planar arrangement of shapes, restricted palette, and focus on the motif of the door, *Hôte* brings to mind Georgia O'Keeffe's series of twenty or so related works painted between 1946 and 1960 referencing the so-called "salita" door in her home in Abiquiú, New Mexico.[6] O'Keeffe's fascination with the "wall with the door in it," as she called it, opened up for her a whole new state of being and artistic innovation that extended her famous early abstractions into new dimensions.[7] Similarly, Yu's formal investigation in 2020 imagines the potential of transforming set image/ground compositions into new permutations. *Hôte* is a prolonged reflection on guest/host negotiations, the dangers of fixed identities in these relationships, and the (im)possibilities offered by a shared positionality held in the French word *hôte*, which can mean both or either host or guest.

After painting only with black for over a decade, Yu felt the need to reassess not only paint's materiality but also its social implications. While researching the subject, she began to make watercolours using a set of four handmade paintstones by Beam Paints, a colour palette inspired by Agnes Martin: black, greys, and blues.[8] Still highly restricted to a limited range of colour, these exploratory beginnings in blueish grey added another layer of complexity to her compositions. During 2021, Yu's reading continued and she made only a few large oils on aluminum, in a range of grey blues. Tangentially referencing the edges and corners of her 2018 series *why does its lock fit my key?* and building on the possibility of the motif of the door, these new paintings introduced a central folded shape — a cuboid coming into being. They gently prepared her for the burst of colour that came during her month-long residency in La Napoule, southeastern France, in April 2022.

It was in a confluence of practical, natural, and artistic circumstances that Yu produced a set of luminous and colourful watercolours later titled the *Inextricably Ours W* series, 2022. A "wonky cuboid" shape, as she refers to it, had appeared

6 Georgia O'Keeffe, *Untitled (Patio Door)*, ca. 1946, Graphite on paper, 43.2 x 35.6 cm, Georgia O'Keeffe Museum, Gift of The Burnett Foundation, 1997.6.3.
7 See Georgiana Uhlyarik, "The 'Light One': A Case Study" in *Georgia O'Keeffe* (London: Tate Publishing, 2016).
8 Anong Beam handmade paintstones from materials harvested on Manitoulin Island, Ontario. Accessed November 25, 2023, https://www.beampaints.com/products/o-keeffe-and-martin-palettes?variant=39291853537349 [Agnes] Martin Palette: Ultra Grey, Payne's Grey, Mars Black and Limestone White. [Agnes] Martin Palette: Ultra Grey, Payne's Grey, Mars Black and Limestone White.

and persisted in her imagination for some time. She had been making line drawing variations of it for months. Trusting that there was great potential in it, Yu responded to the extraordinary quality of light of the Mediterranean coast by allowing herself to use the full range of colours in the Holbein watercolour set she had brought for ease of portability. She spent the month composing different permutations of this shapeshifting cuboid. Sometimes its facets are different tones of one colour: orange, yellow, blue. In others it is multicoloured in related hues. Her marks are visible, even, revealing the layers and method of application. The facets are translucent, yet also distinct, making the shape recede and protrude at once. Edges are not drawn lines; rather they are the result of facets encountering one another. The surrounding colour varies between high contrast with the central image — as in green and yellow (*W22-05* P.32) — and subtle shifts, sometimes of oranges (*W22-01* P.33) or blues (*W22-02* P.33).

These dynamic and compelling watercolours are ever changing. Working and reworking the facets, the colours, the pattern of strokes, and the compositions, Yu is attempting to resist a tiered figure/ground relationship. "I had this idea to flatten hierarchical subordination," she said, seeking to create a shared space of balance, of simply being in relation to one another. Her cuboids hover in an in-between state of suggested solidity and boundless permeability. Each suggests its own state of becoming; viewed together, they create a syncopated rhythm of radiating shapes and colours, mutating, interrelated yet coherent.

Once back in her painting studio, Yu began exploring in oil on aluminum (her chosen support material since 2004) the ways in which her watercolours had articulated new pictorial directions. *Inextricably Ours 22-01, 2022* P.27, is a cuboid with orange, red, and ochre facets in a field of green overlayed with faint orange streaks. The green at once radiates out and encircles the cuboid, and reads as an autonomous plane extending beyond the edge of the painting. The six edges of the form delineate the central shape and place it in complementary contrast with the green. The brushstrokes of each facet are visible, wispy, layered, and belaboured, yet appear effortless. They are carefully organized and directional, implying an internal logic or system. The facets can be read as separate, or in a variety of combinations — as two adjacent triangles can perceptually conjoin into a quadrilateral with two different tonalities thus creating depth. On its own, the uniform colour of each facet insists on the flatness of its shape. Taken together, they create a state of in between and all at once. Each facet in the image may be distinct in colour or direction of stroke, yet the composition coalesces into an

Inextricably Ours 22-01, 2022
oil on aluminium | huile sur aluminium
153 × 140 cm

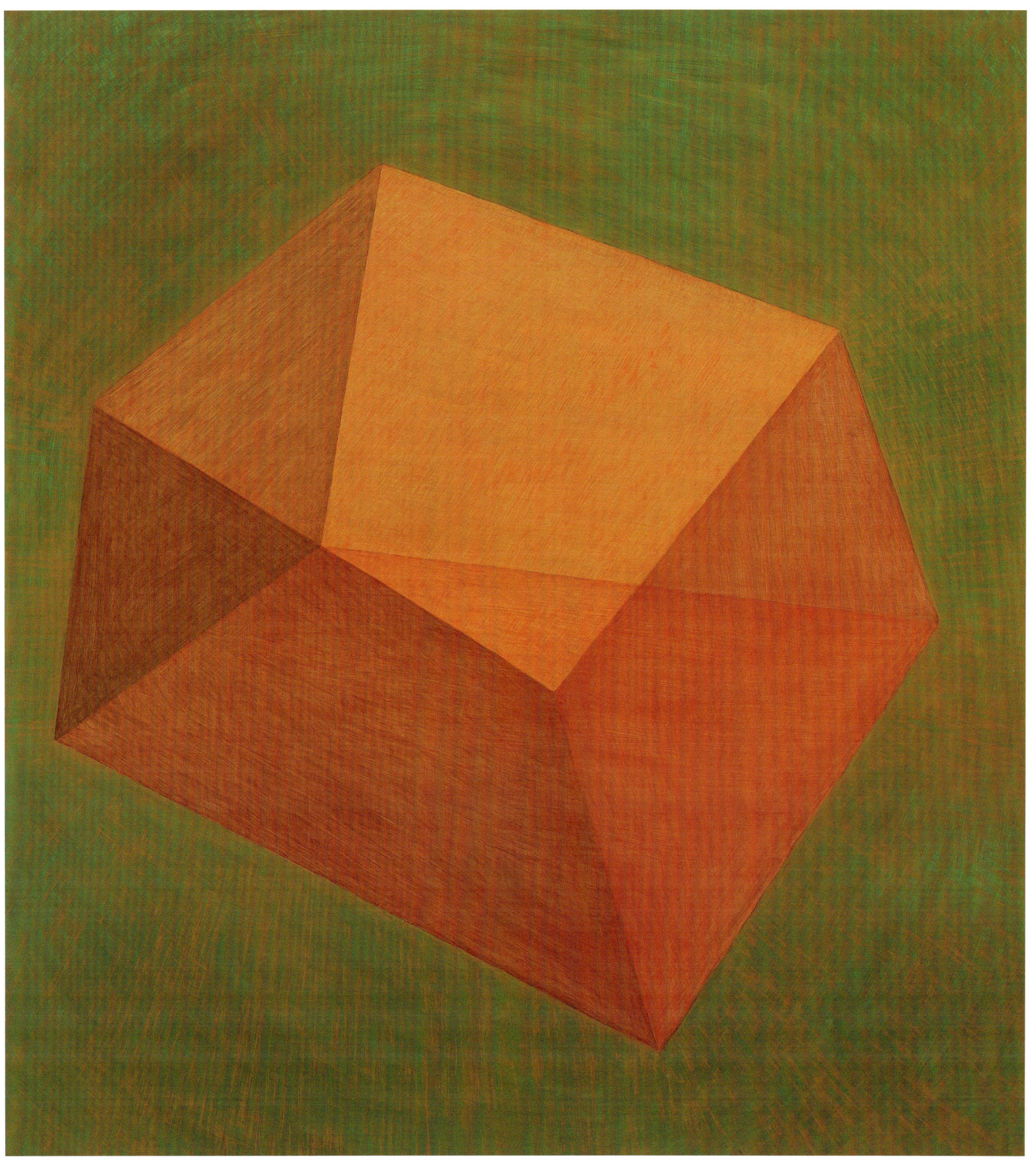

all-overness through her even-handed application of medium. The cuboid is an active but contained shape with edges that never quite sharpen, are never quite in focus. Yu produces an interplay of geometric shapes that bend in and out and then regroup anew. In each of the paintings from this period, there is a passage where the eye can rest longer, and be fed, before the direction of the brushstrokes journeys again in and around the composition.

Yu works on several paintings at a time, allowing each layer to dry before applying the next. This process is well suited for her open-ended project, as it allows new ideas to fold into earlier compositions. In this series, paint covers the whole sheet of metal in varying degrees of translucency, thus controlling the reflectivity of the aluminum in the painting. In a work such as *Inextricably Ours 23-03*, 2023 P. 44, the aluminum seeps through several facets of the cuboid, in contrast with the opaqueness of the expanse that contains it. In her watercolours, the light emanates from within, while in the oils the reflection of the surrounding light activates their luminosity. While some of the paintings reference one of the watercolours and others are newly conceived compositions, working with oil on a much larger scale renegotiates the figure's relationship to the ground.

The nearly monochromatic cadmium red paintings from 2023 — *Inextricably Ours 23-02* P. 29, *Inextricably Ours 23-03* P. 44, and *Inextricably Ours 23-04* P. 37 — confound the planar interrelationship between the cuboid and the plane. While still somewhat delineated spaces, they are brought together to be one and both at the same time. Aesthetically generous and inviting, these red compositions are self-propagating, iterative, and complete, and in relation to one another. A new dimension appears in *Inextricably Ours 23-04* P. 37. Three lines, originating in one point of the cuboid, extend beyond its shape, reaching the edge of the sheet metal, one meeting the bottom left corner of the painting. These extensions activate a different scale and claim the space beyond the painting itself as part of the composition. The lines connect in multiple ways to each other and produce several interrelationships. The red has spawned shades beyond itself. Shapes appear, dissolve, and stay, patiently taking turns. They scale up and out and inward and down. It is not that the composition is unstable, but rather it is much more constantly shapeshifting, marking the beginning of the opening of the cuboid. Yu starts from that limitation without predetermination, "to see what happens," and to open up possibilities instead of closing them down.

Inextricably Ours 23-02, 2023
oil on aluminium | huile sur aluminium
153 × 140 cm

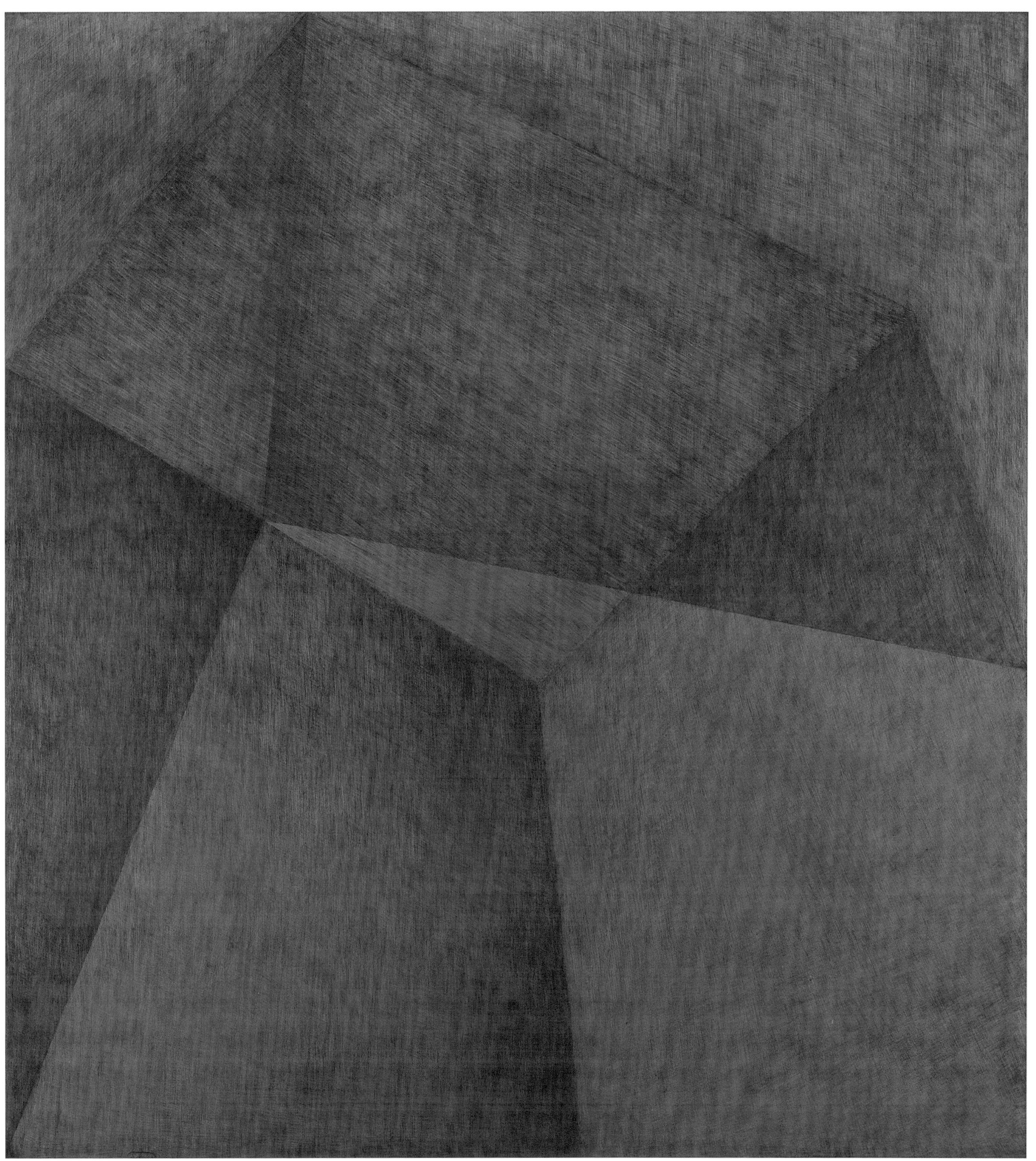

Inextricably Ours 23-01, 2023
oil on aluminium | huile sur aluminium
153 × 140 cm

Working in her Berlin studio in early 2023, Yu experimented with Caran d'Ache gouaches to push open the cuboids in this materially seductive, velvety medium. In her *Inextricably Ours* G series, 2023, she experiments with extending the colour planes towards the edges of the paper, zooming in while also opening up new dimensions. No longer contained, these compositions appear less stable, as though they are in the very act of mutating. They are myriad colours — green, blue, yellow, red, orange, purple — creating a variety of interrelated oblongs and polygons. Seen together, the planes of colour extend from one sheet to the next, compositionally connecting in the viewer's space.

Inextricably Ours 23-04 P. 37 was reworked from an earlier state following the gouache drawings. Back in her painting studio in Ottawa, Yu began to work through this approach in a new set of paintings, as well as push those she had yet to finish. *Inextricably Ours 23-05* P. 35, *Inextricably Ours 23-06* P. 38, *Inextricably Ours 23-07* P. 34, and *Inextricably Ours 23-08* P. 39 are conceived in this new manner — planes no longer predictable, scale no longer perceivable but rather intuited, colours abundant. These potent images make themselves present without referent or inner hierarchy, creating and recreating interrelationships, negotiating and sharing their space as both hosts and guests at once.

The labour in the studio is the labour of imagination. Jinny Yu's painting practice is compelling in its subtlety and restraint. Deeply philosophical, her work is poetically political and quietly beautiful. Like all engaged artists, Yu takes from the fullness of the world around her what most resonates with relevance for her, and transforms a gesture, a material, an image, or a thought into an immersive journey into her consciousness, her state of mind. She invites us to walk into her fragments of thought as they reveal themselves piecemeal and all at once — to always slow down and ruminate on contradictions suspended ethereally, not to be resolved but rather absorbed. Her ability to parse fine and poignant distinctions is what reveals her as highly attuned to power dynamics and possessing a sensitive and resonating membrane through which to process and perceive. ■

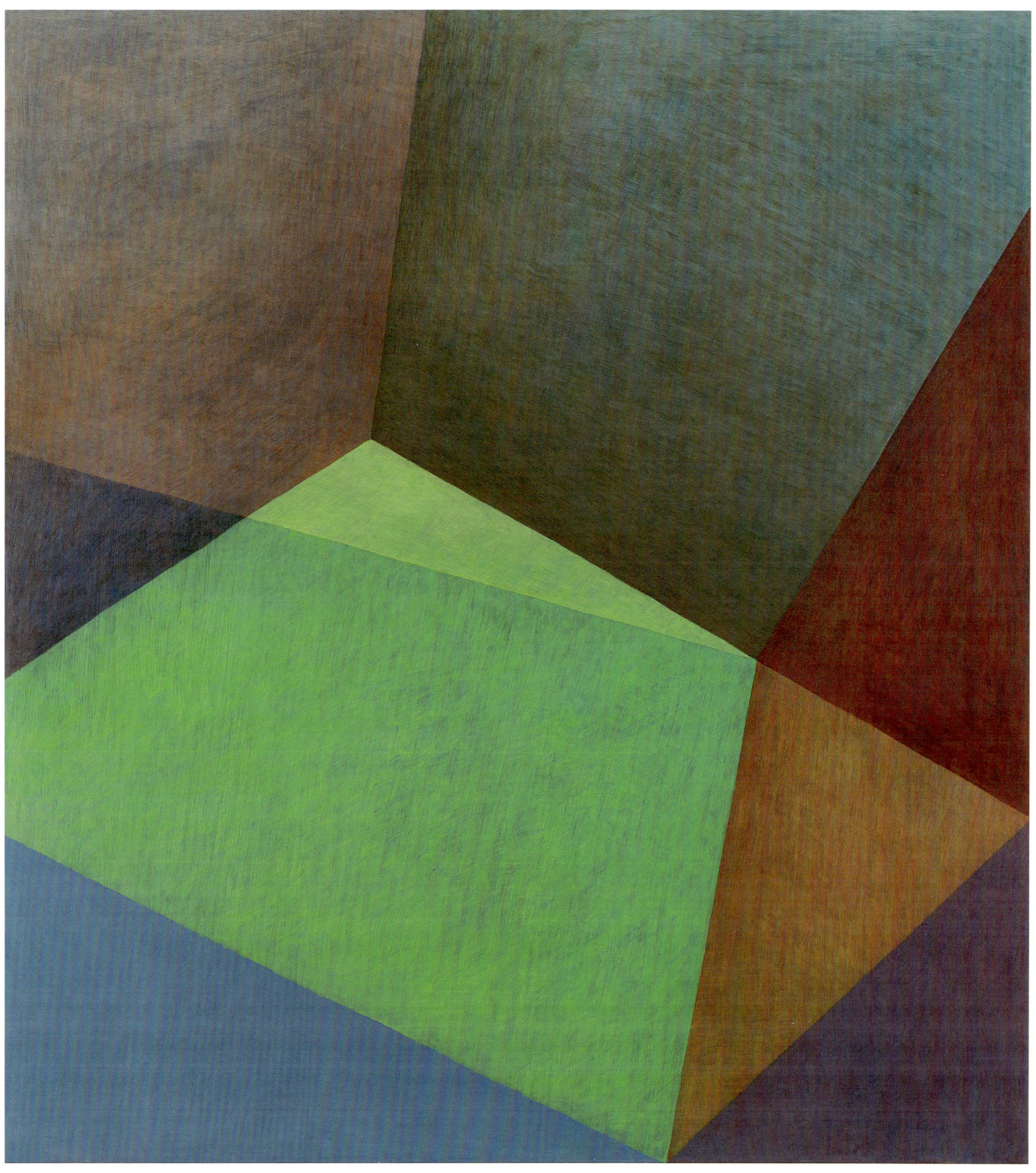

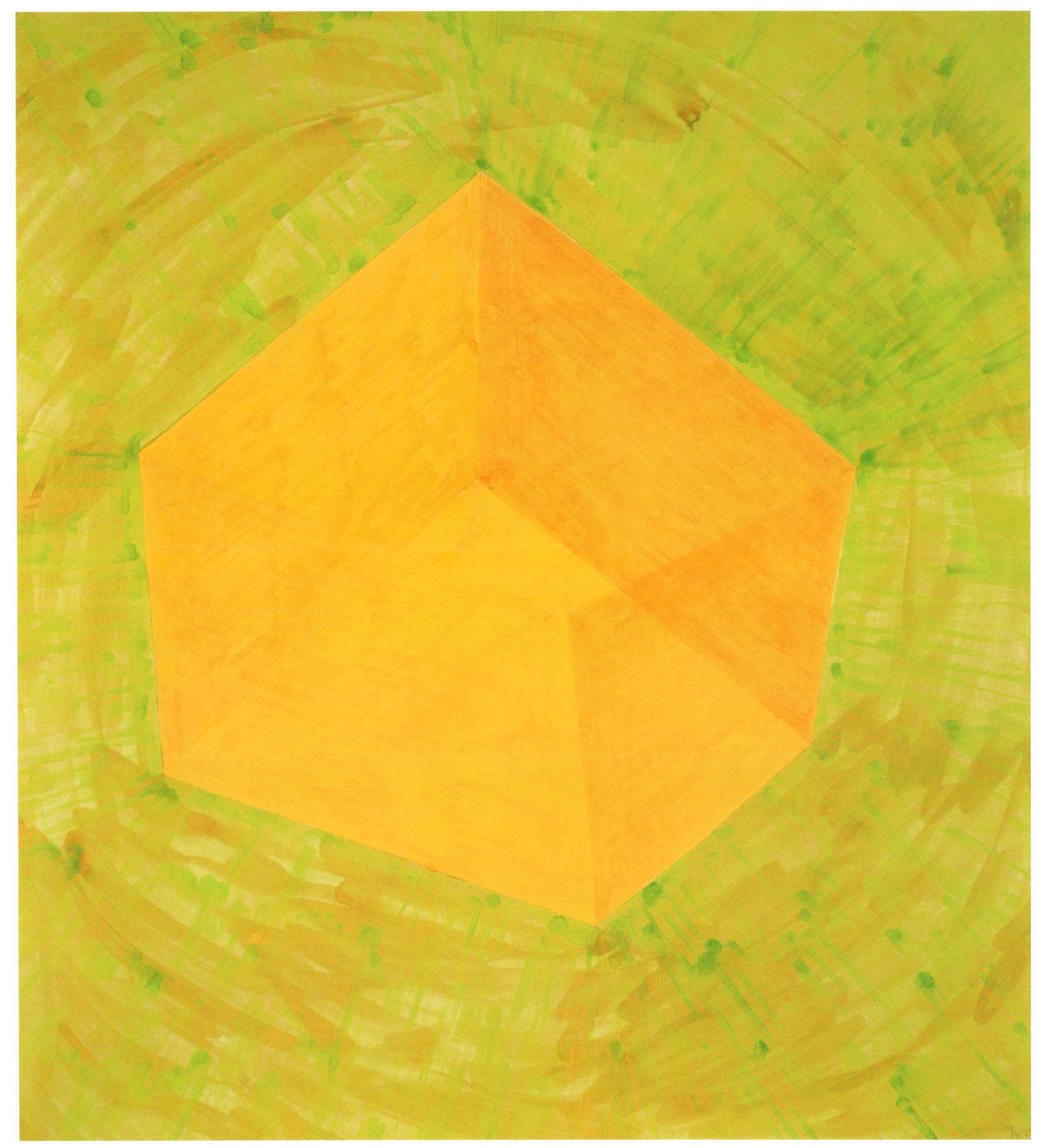

Inextricably Ours W22-05, 2022
watercolour on paper | aquarelle sur papier
48 × 44 cm

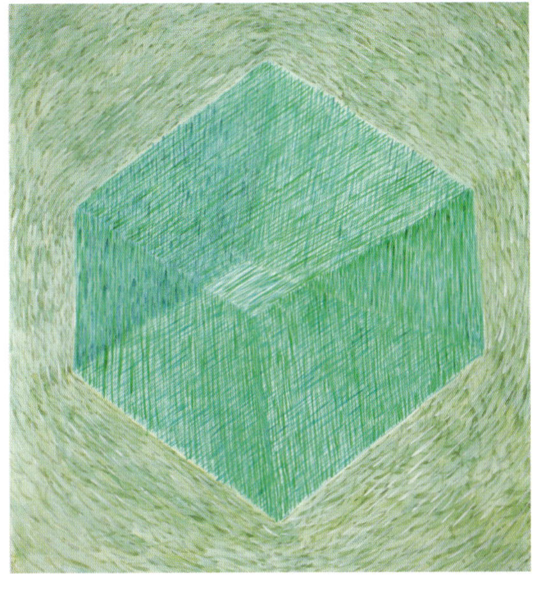

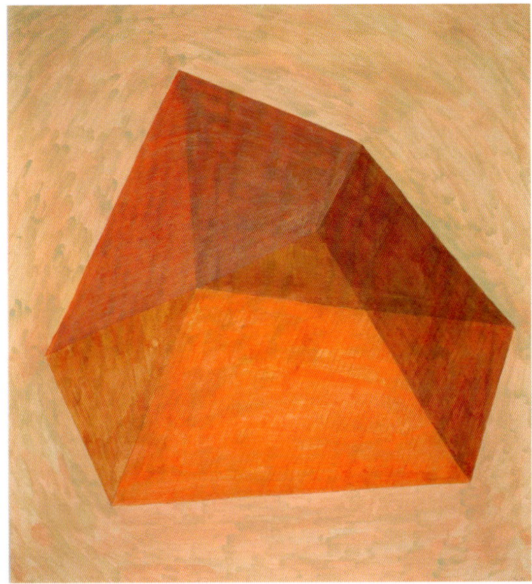

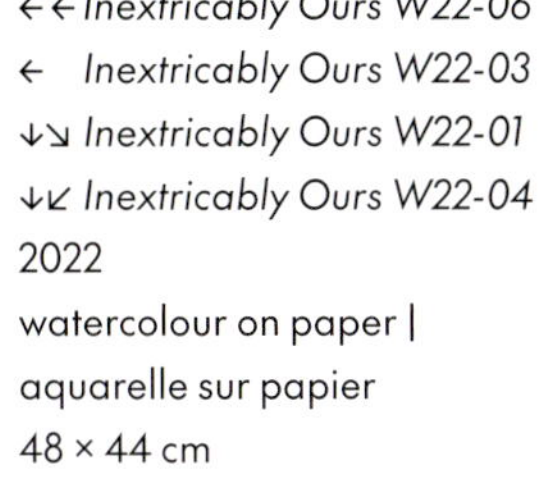

←← *Inextricably Ours W22-06*
← *Inextricably Ours W22-03*
↓↘ *Inextricably Ours W22-01*
↓↙ *Inextricably Ours W22-04*
2022
watercolour on paper |
aquarelle sur papier
48 × 44 cm

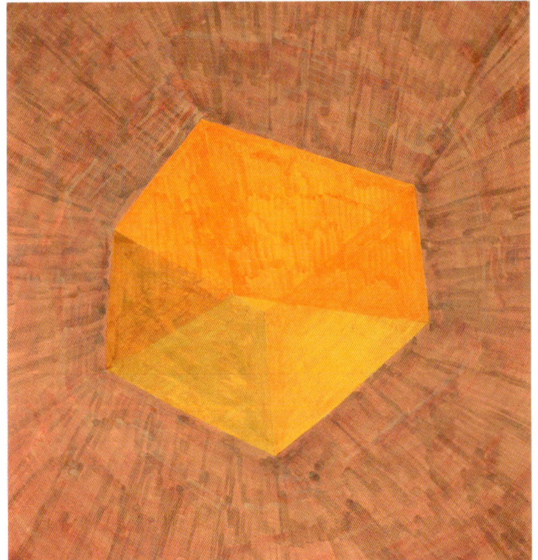

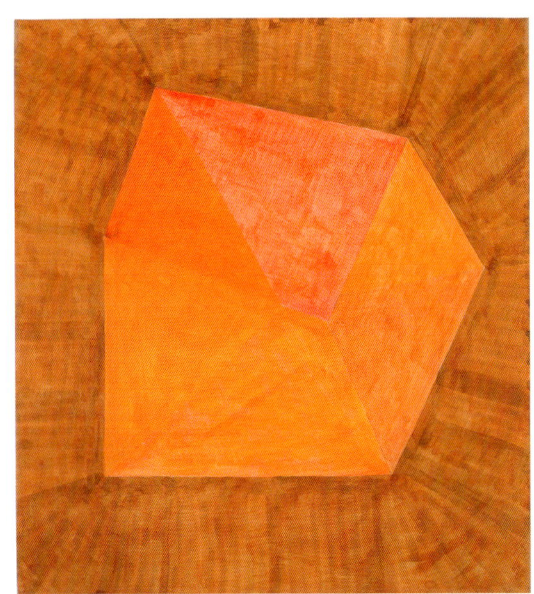

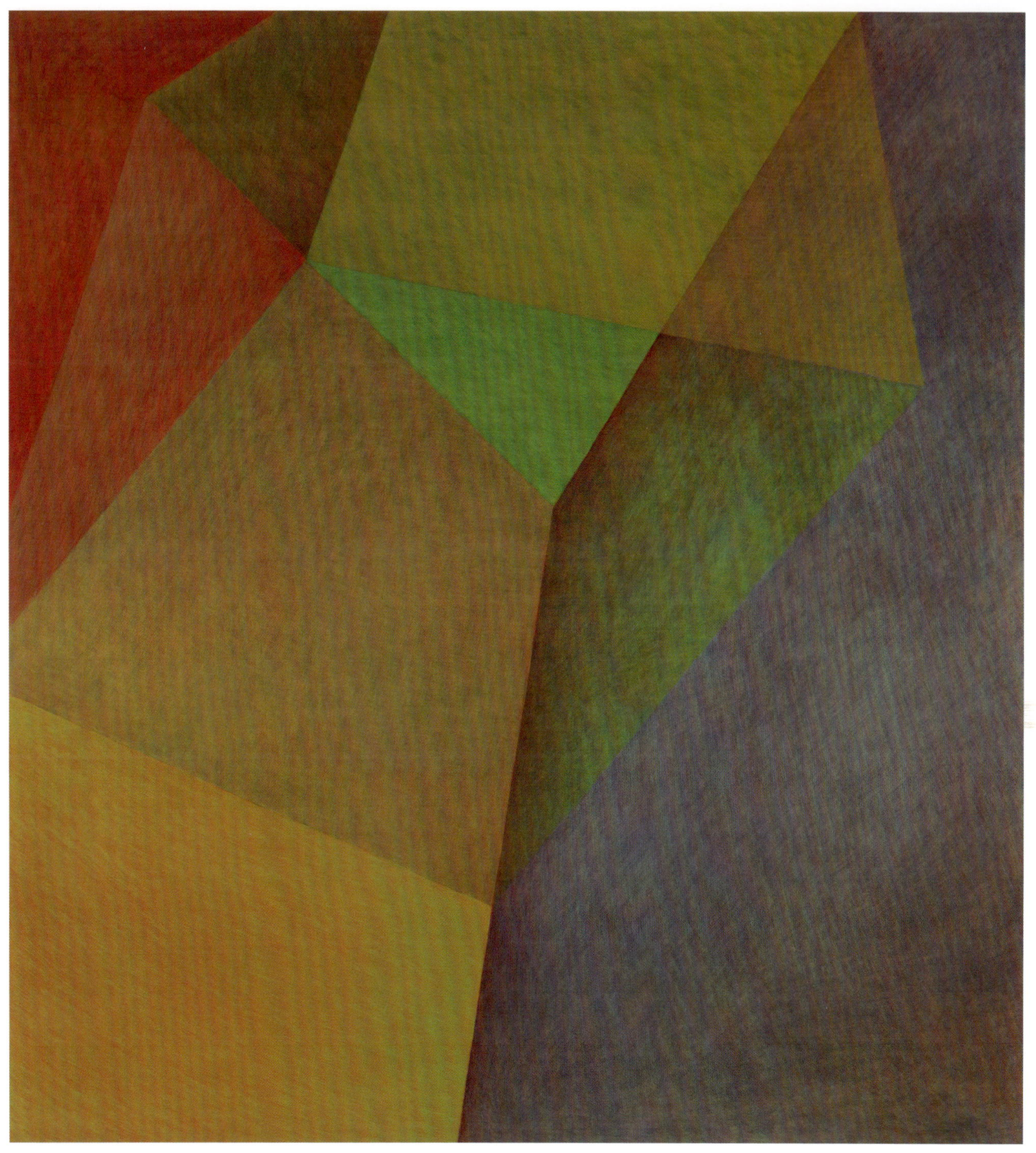

Inextricably Ours 23-07, 2023
oil on aluminium | huile sur aluminium
153 × 140 cm

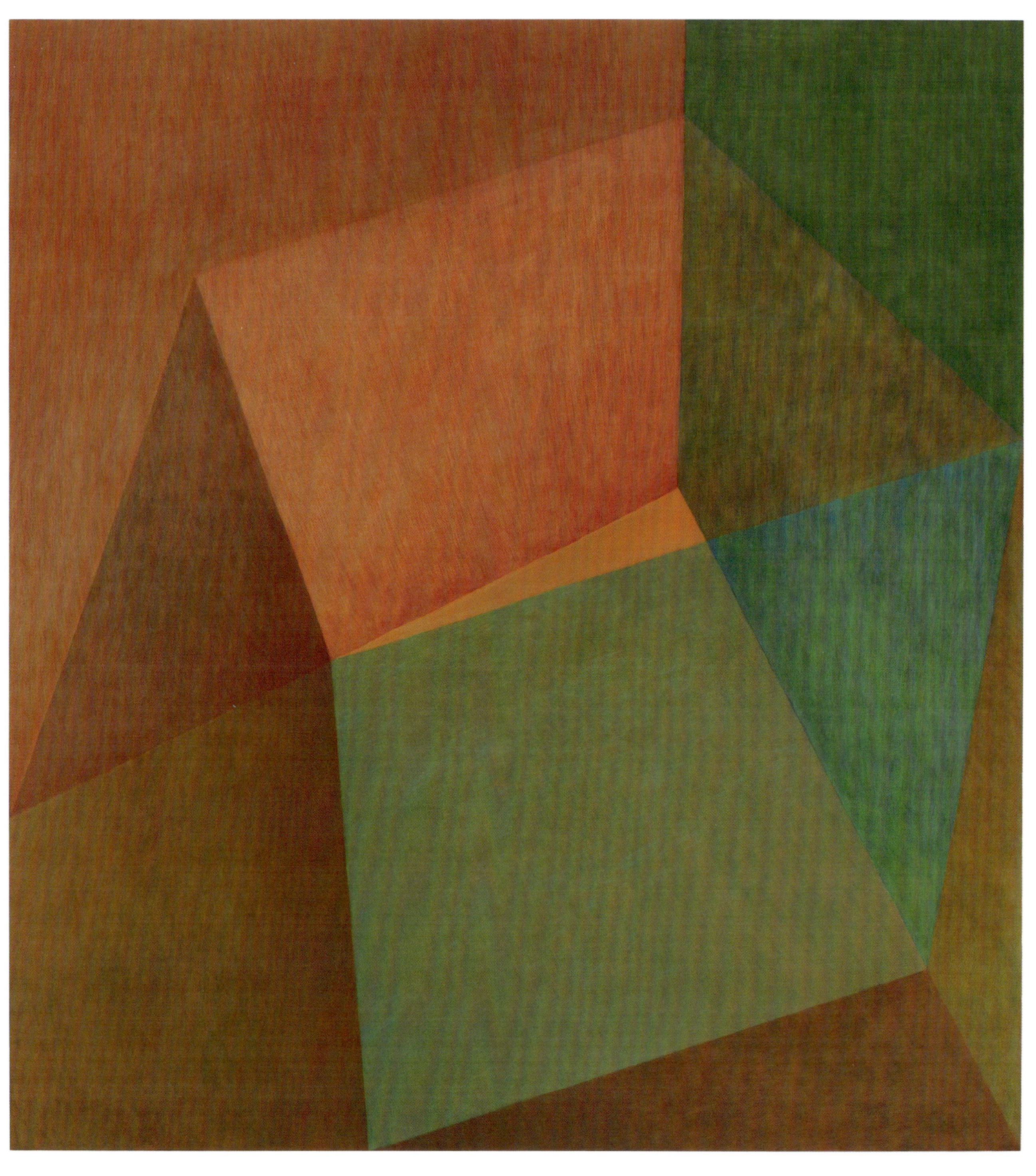

Inextricably Ours 23-05, 2023
oil on aluminium | huile sur aluminium
153 × 140 cm

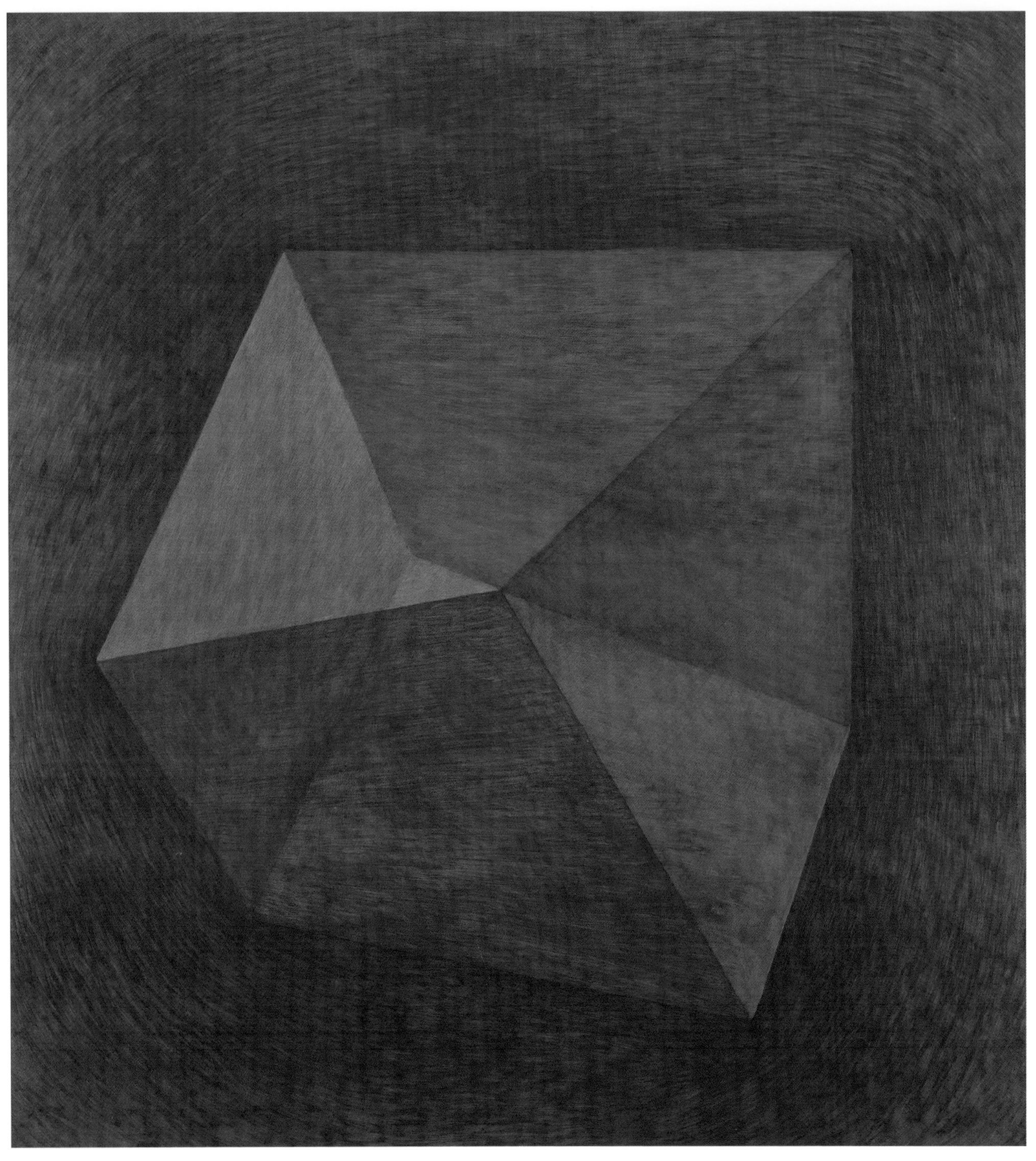

Inextricably Ours 22-05, 2023
oil on aluminium | huile sur aluminium
153 × 140 cm
Private collection | collection privée

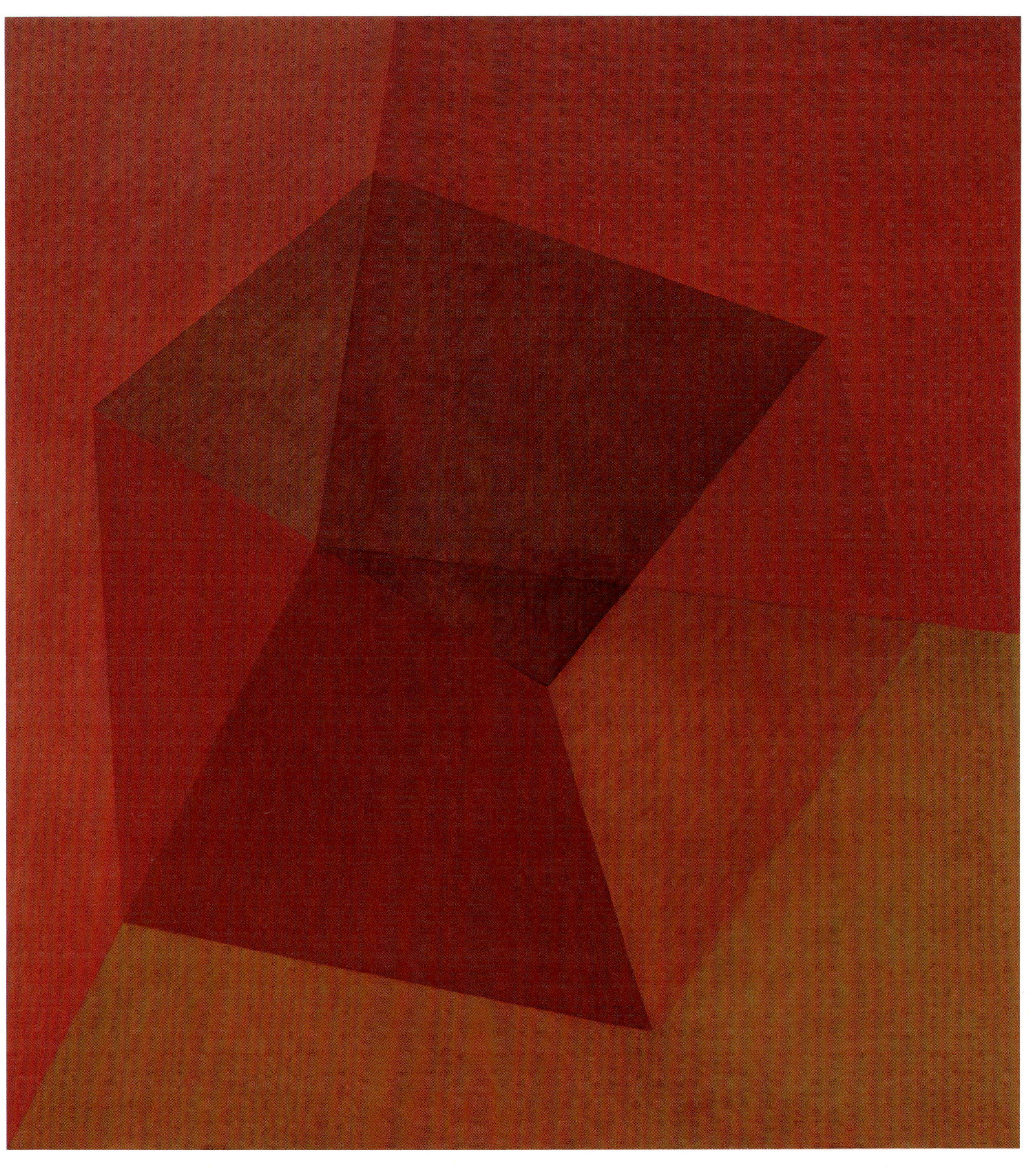

Inextricably Ours 23-04, 2023
oil on aluminium | huile sur aluminium
153 × 140 cm

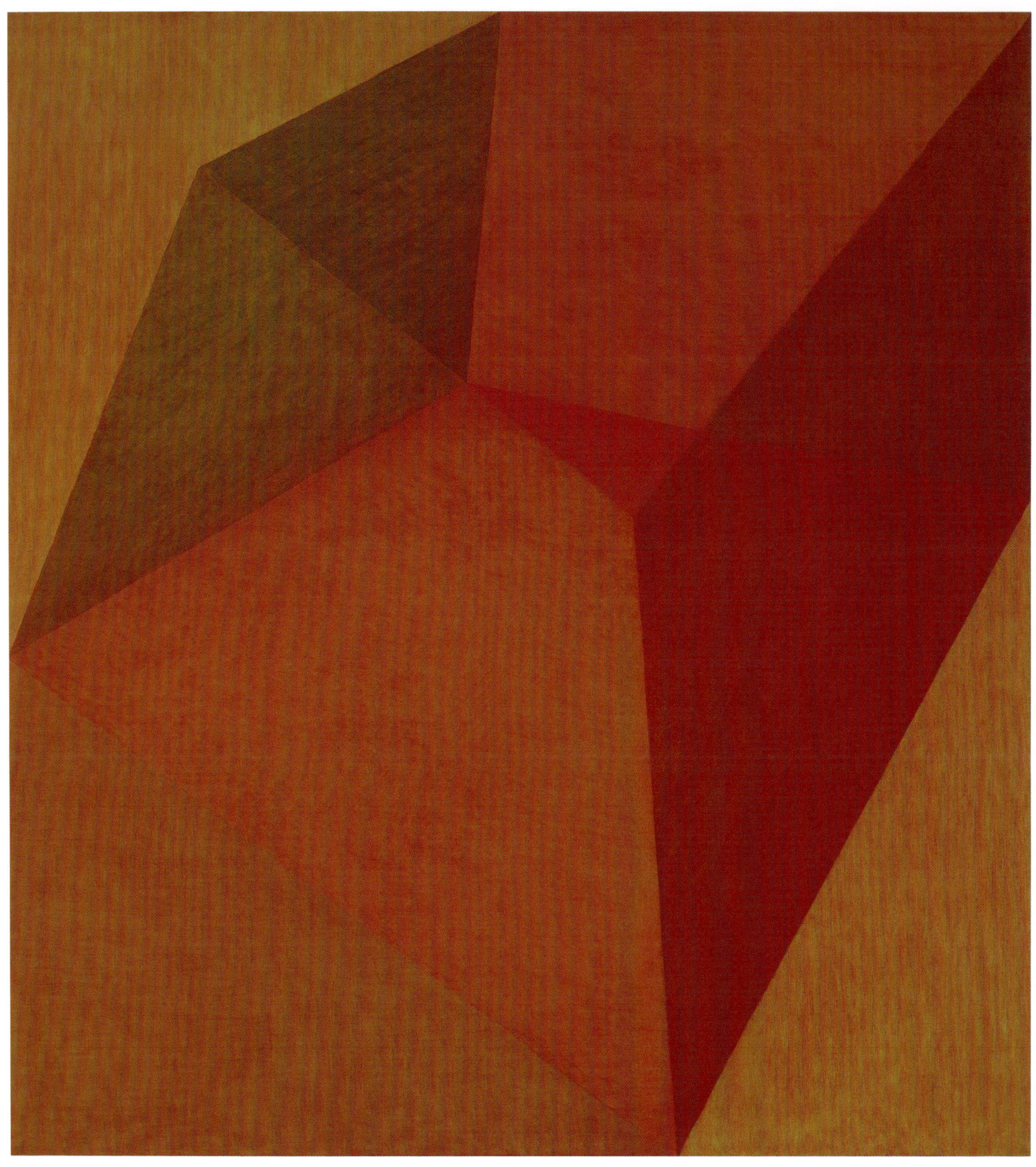

Inextricably Ours 23-06, 2023
oil on aluminium | huile sur aluminium
153 × 140 cm

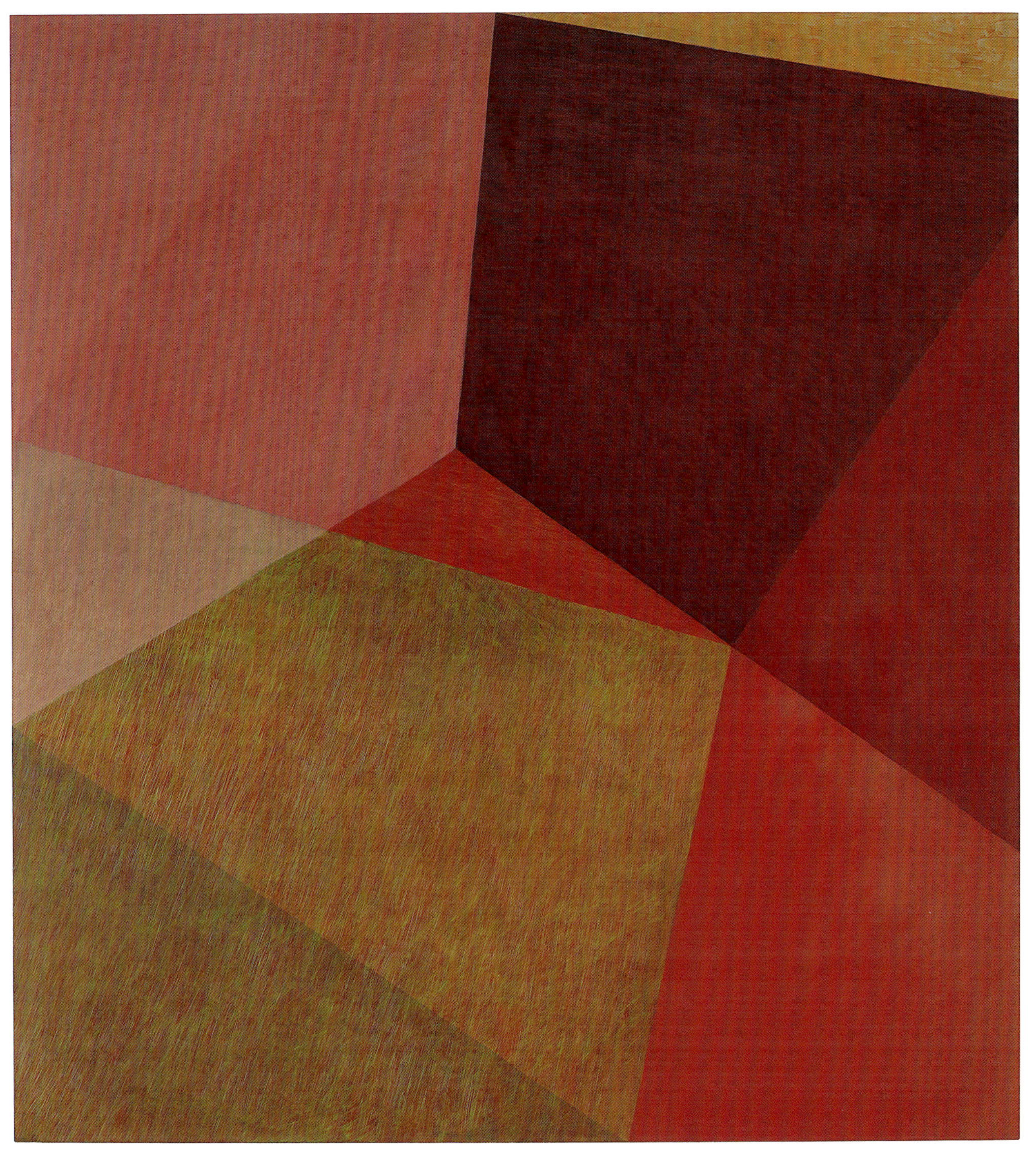

Inextricably Ours 23-08, 2023
oil on aluminium | huile sur aluminium
153 × 140 cm

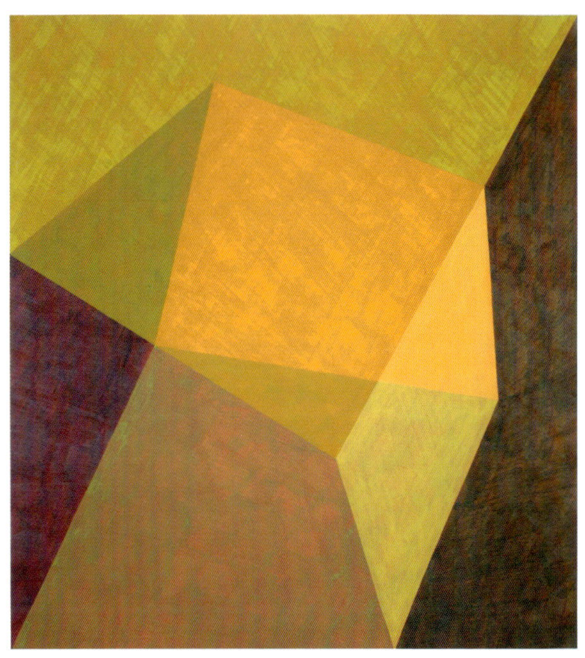

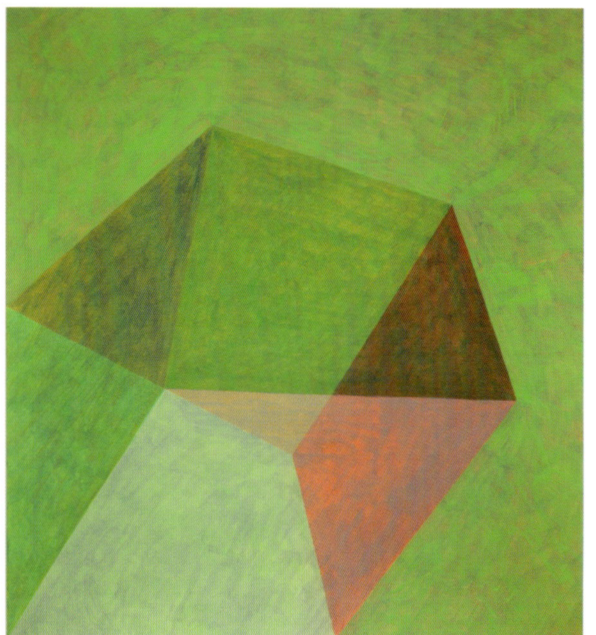

↑ *Inextricably Ours G23-03*
↗ *Inextricably Ours G23-06*
→ *Inextricably Ours G23-07*
2023
gouache on paper | gouache sur papier
55 × 50 cm

↓ Installation view | vue d'installation
JINNY YU: AT ONCE
June 22, 2024 – January 5, 2025 |
22 juin 2024 – 5 janvier 2025
Art Gallery of Ontario | Musée
des beaux-arts de l'Ontario, Toronto

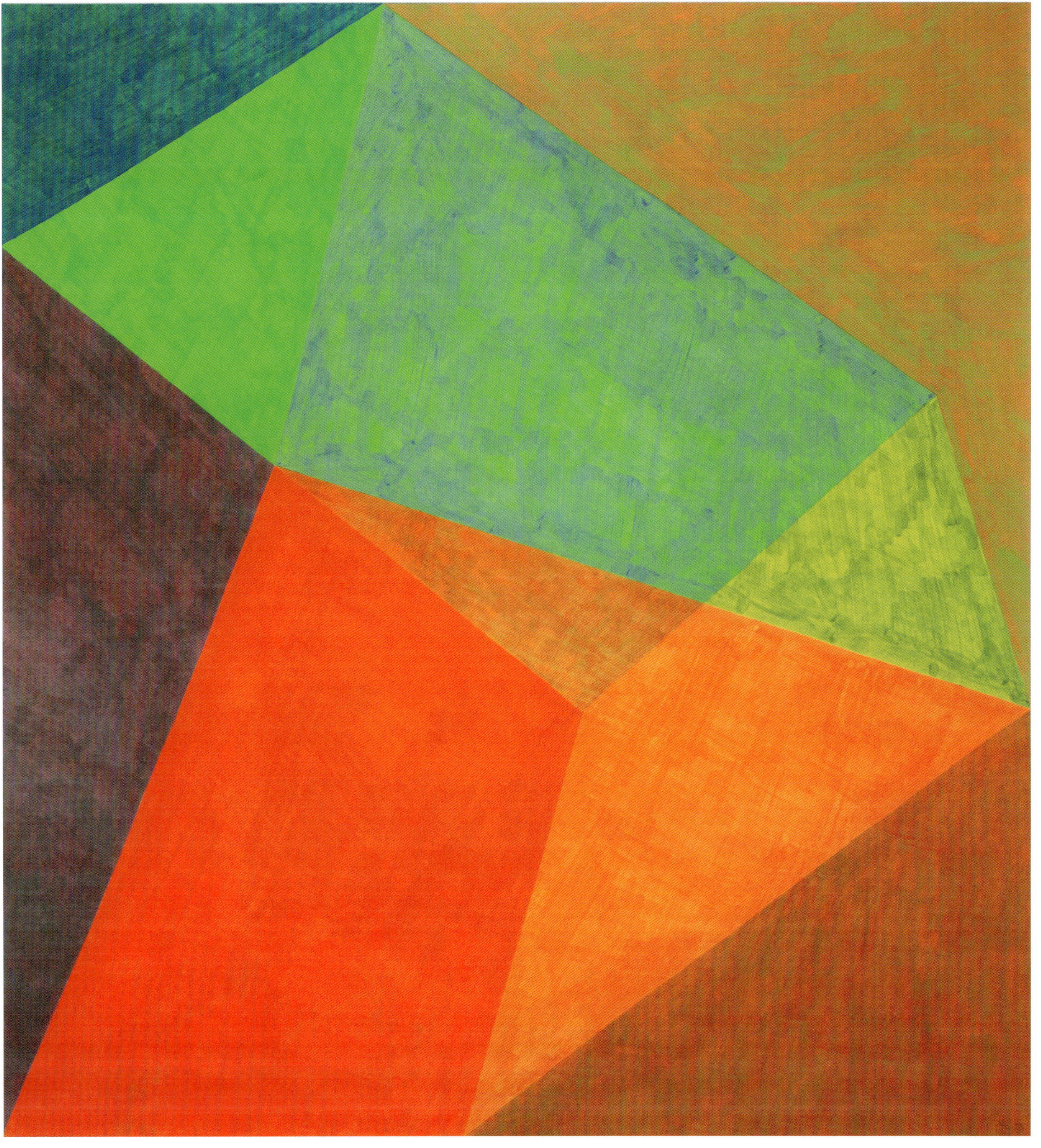

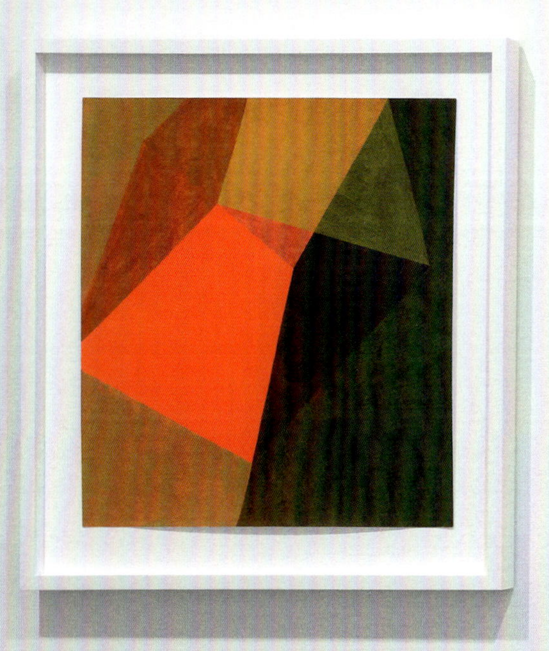
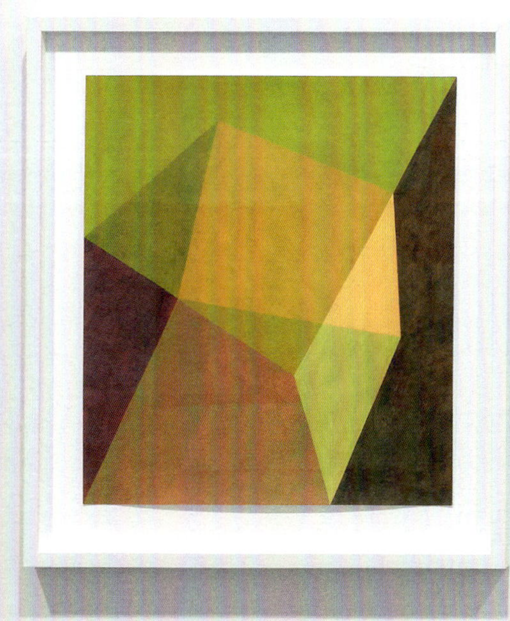
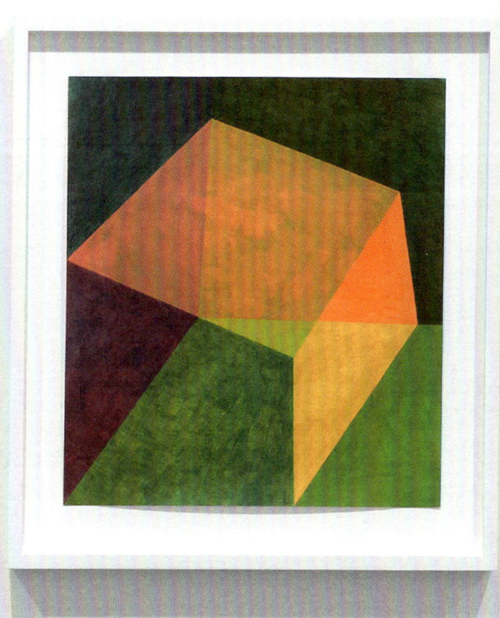

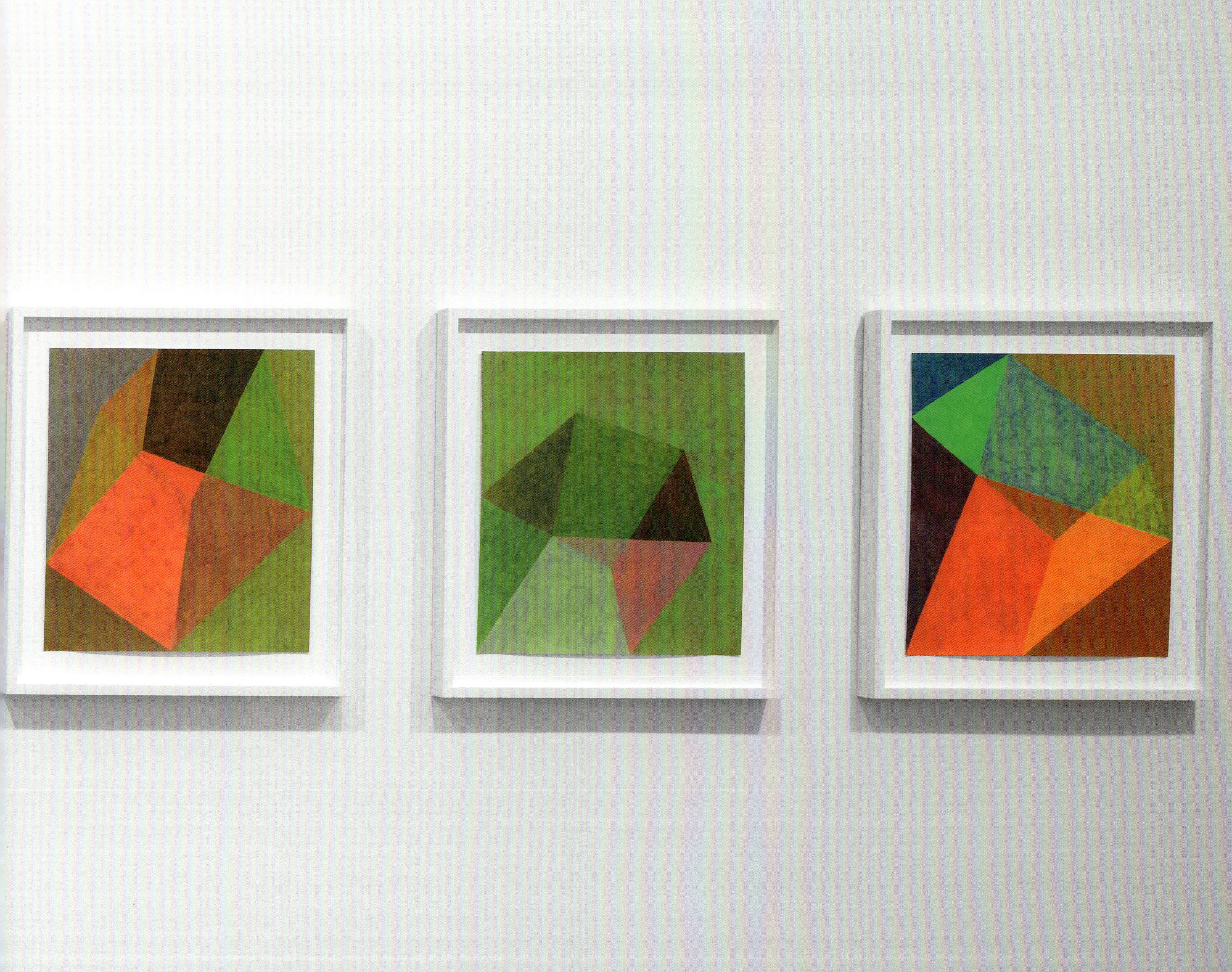

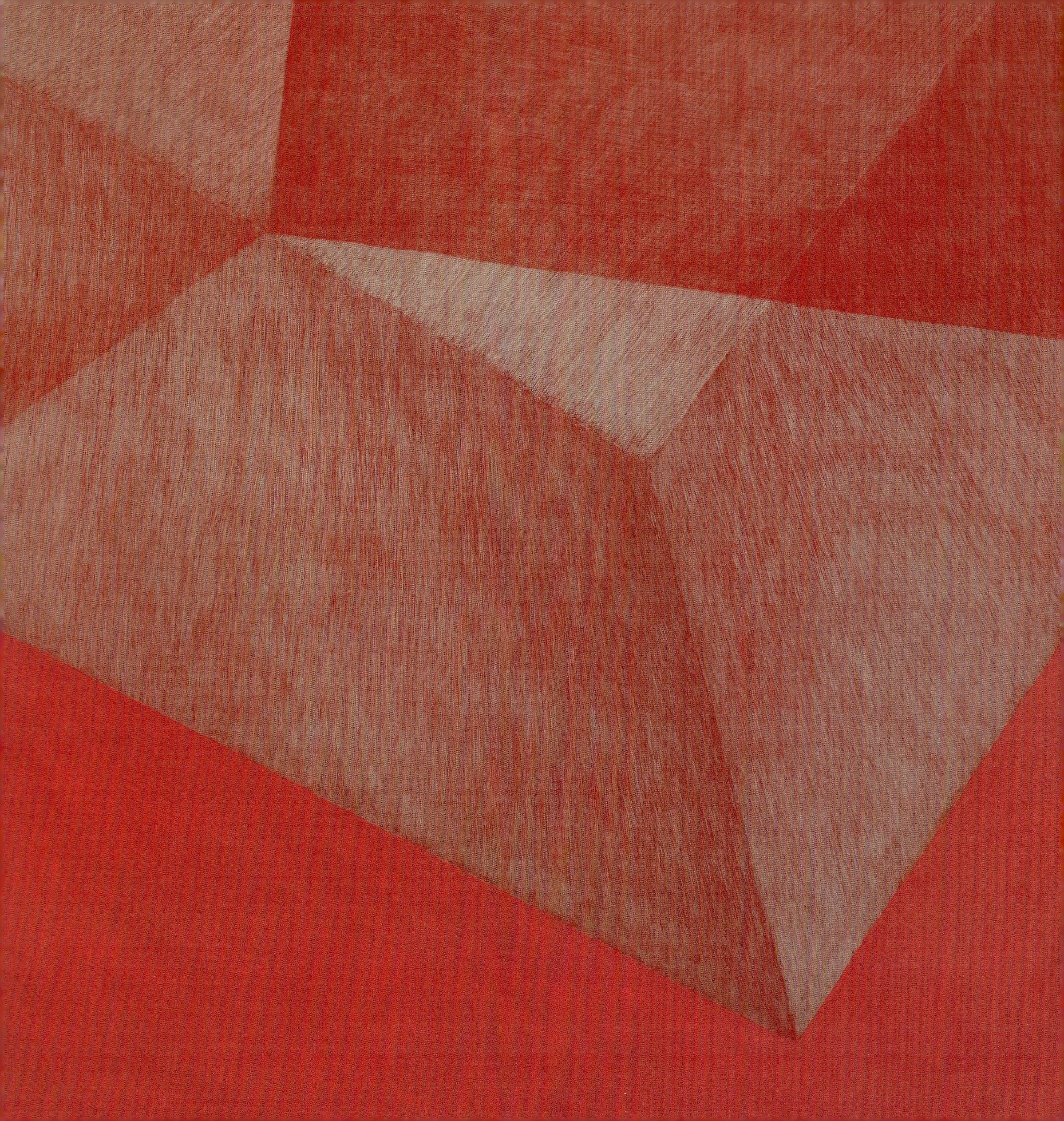

J'écris pendant les trois jours de Chuseok, le festival coréen de la récolte d'automne, et quelques jours seulement après l'équinoxe d'automne de 2023, lorsque la lumière et l'obscurité divisent la journée en deux autour de la planète. C'est un moment où le soleil apparaît directement au-dessus de l'équateur terrestre, équilibrant les deux hémisphères alors qu'ils entament leur voyage à venir, étendant leur portée sur le jour ou la nuit de l'autre hémisphère. C'est également la troisième fois que le Canada célèbre la Journée nationale de la vérité et de la réconciliation, qui a lieu le 30 septembre de chaque année depuis 2021 – une journée de commémoration et de réflexion sur l'histoire violente et injuste du colonialisme dans ces territoires, et sur notre responsabilité collective de rechercher la vérité et la justice pour les peuples autochtones et d'honorer leur souveraineté.

C'est à l'occasion de la rencontre de ces événements apparemment distincts, mais pourtant enchevêtrés que les nouvelles peintures et œuvres sur papier colorées et kaléidoscopiques de Jinny Yu ont pu être contextualisées. Ces dernières années, Yu a développé de nouveaux intérêts de recherche, en prenant conscience de nouvelles complexités concernant les notions d'appartenance à un lieu, un état d'apatridie et d'acceptation du déplacement en tant que condition humaine. La nuance de « ne pas avoir de lieu d'appartenance du tout, plutôt que ne pas pouvoir s'appartenir[1] » est peut-être mince, mais elle constitue une différence essentielle pour faire évoluer la compréhension de la possibilité d'établir des liens et du poids imposant des événements historiques.

Inextricably Ours 23-03 (detail | détail), 2023
oil on aluminium | huile sur aluminium
153 × 140 cm

* *Comme toujours, je tiens à remercier Ihor Holubizky pour ses conversations sinueuses et sans fin sur l'art, les artistes et l'acte créatif, parmi beaucoup d'autres choses.*

1 Sauf indication contraire, toutes les citations de l'artiste proviennent d'une discussion avec l'artiste à son atelier à Ottawa le 14 août 2023.

Hôte XLII, 2020
graphite on paper | graphite sur papier
42 × 42 cm
Montreal Museum of Fine Arts Collection |
Collection du Musée des beaux-arts
de Montréal

Les œuvres de sa nouvelle série, *Inextricably Ours*, représentent un voyage de près de trois ans de recherche, de peinture et de plusieurs résidences d'artistes, au cours desquelles elle a remis en question et réexaminé la «binarité de l'état d'hôte et d'invité», en réajustant son langage pictural de l'abstraction.[2] Comme le dit Yu, après *Perpetual Guest* (2019) – son installation de peinture sur verre – et *Hôte* (2020) – ses dessins et son livre d'artiste – elle a voulu s'attarder plus longuement sur la relation trouble invité/hôte, et remettre en question les limites de ces positions établies.

Yu a entrepris de réaliser des peintures qui prennent du temps, qui sont laborieuses, méticuleuses et ouvertes, sans savoir où elles pourraient mener. Au cours des 14 dernières années, son travail s'est inscrit dans un domaine conceptuel où elle «questionnait qu'est-ce que la peinture, au-delà de l'image[3]». Pour elle, peindre était une action qui constitue un tableau, un geste, un coup de pinceau mécanique. Une série de questions artistiques préoccupantes, associées à des événements sociaux mondiaux troublants et à une profonde réflexion personnelle, ont amené Yu à reconsidérer le rôle indéniablement générateur de l'image dans la peinture. Une forme est apparue dans ses dessins et, avec elle, son incontournable «problème du fond», comme elle l'appelle. Peu de temps après – peut-être inévitablement – son œuvre a accueilli à nouveau, avec toute sa force, une explosion de la couleur.

Le voyage de trois ans de Yu a commencé lentement et sensiblement à la fin de l'année 2020. L'artiste s'efforçait de faire face à la pandémie de COVID-19 en cours et à son amplification du racisme anti-asiatique, ainsi qu'à l'agitation civile croissante condamnant la discrimination raciale systémique. Plus tôt dans l'année, elle avait produit et exposé *Hôte*, 42 dessins au graphite – un ensemble résultant d'une tâche pratiquée quotidiennement – qu'elle avait transformé en livre d'artiste.[4] Conçue pour être vue de manière séquentielle, la série débute par un grand rectangle sombre placé au centre d'un carré vierge. La relation figure/fond suggère la position invité/hôte. La combinaison de trois mots guidait sa réflexion : «L'invité peut-il être l'hôte? L'hôte peut-il être l'invité? L'invité peut

2 Texte d'exposition de 2023 pour *JINNY YU : AT ONCE* à Musée des beaux-arts de l'Ontario, Toronto (22 juin, 2024 – 5 janvier, 2025). Archives de l'artiste.

3 Citation de l'artiste dans *Jinny Yu : to activate space* (Montréal: Éditions Art Mûr, 2014), p. 43.

4 Pour plus d'informations sur *Hôte*, voir https://artmur.com/en/artists/jinny-yu/hote/ et voir la présentation du livre d'artiste *HÔTE* (2021), produit par le Korean Cultural Centre https://www.youtube.com/watch?v=4n33OcjDCls. *Hôte* fait désormais partie de la collection du Musée des beaux-arts de Montréal.

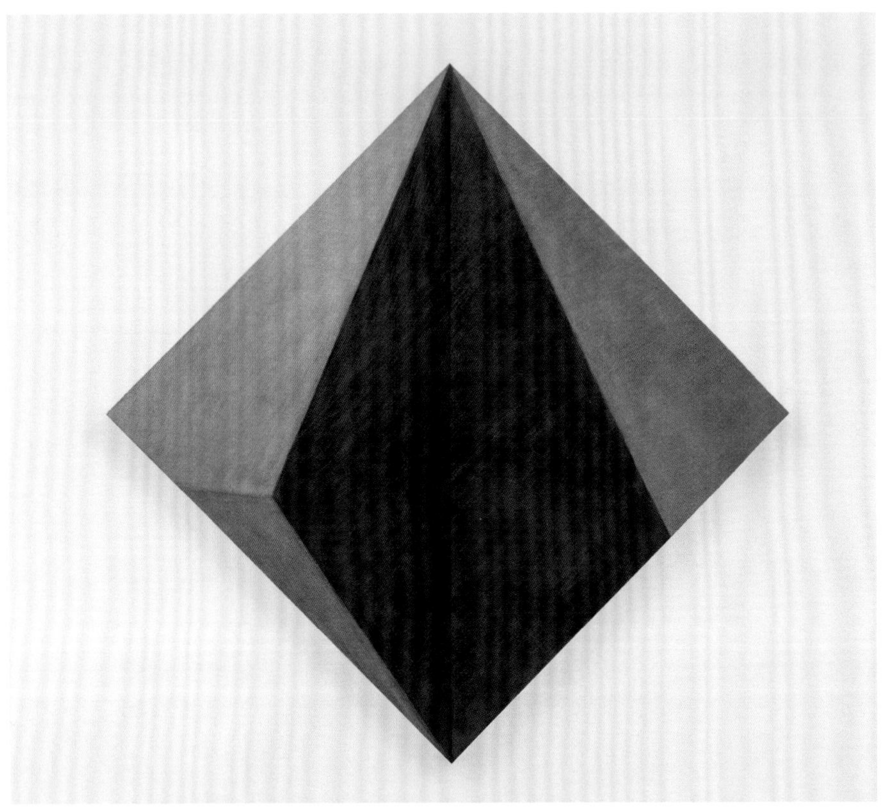

why does its lock fit my key?, 2018
oil on aluminium | huile sur aluminium
86 × 86 cm

why does its lock fit my key?, 2018
oil on aluminium | huile sur aluminium
66 × 66 cm

recevoir. L'hôte peut être invité.[5]» À chaque nouveau dessin, la relation entre l'espace dessiné et le blanc de la feuille est reconstituée. Au fil de la série, des hachures gris clair et gris foncé apparaissent dans des compositions de gris sur gris et finissent par occuper la totalité de la page, brouillant les positions et ouvrant des possibilités. Plus loin, le rectangle est placé à un angle aigu – peut-être une porte légèrement entrouverte – ce qui évoque une troisième dimension. La série se termine par une feuille couverte de hachures à la mine de plomb, au centre de laquelle se trouve un espace très étroit et vertical laissé nu, à l'exception d'une fine ligne au centre P. 46.

Par sa simplicité formelle, la disposition plane des formes, la palette restreinte et l'attention mise sur le motif de la porte, *Hôte* rappelle la série d'une vingtaine d'œuvres connexes de Georgia O'Keeffe, peintes entre 1946 et 1960 et faisant référence à la porte dite «salita» de sa maison d'Abiquiú, au Nouveau-Mexique.[6] La fascination d'O'Keeffe pour le «mur avec la porte», comme elle l'appelait, lui a ouvert un tout nouvel état d'esprit et d'innovation artistique qui a propulsé ses célèbres premières abstractions vers de nouvelles dimensions.[7] De même, la recherche formelle de Yu en 2020 imagine le potentiel de transformer des compositions image/fond en de nouvelles permutations. *Hôte* est une réflexion prolongée sur les négociations hôte/invité, les dangers des identités fixes dans ces relations et les (im)possibilités offertes par une position partagée contenue dans le mot français hôte, qui peut signifier à la fois hôte et invité, soit l'un ou l'autre.

Après avoir peint uniquement en noir pendant plus de dix ans, Yu a ressenti le besoin de réévaluer non seulement la matérialité de la peinture, mais aussi ses implications sociales. Tout en faisant des recherches sur le sujet, elle a commencé à réaliser des aquarelles en utilisant un ensemble de quatre pierres à peindre fabriquées à la main par Beam Paints, une palette de couleurs inspirée par Agnès Martin : noirs, gris et bleus.[8] Encore très limités à une gamme de couleurs restreinte, ces débuts exploratoires en gris bleuté ont ajouté une nouvelle couche de complexité à ses compositions. Au cours de l'année 2021, Yu poursuivit ses lectures et ne réalisa que quelques grandes huiles sur aluminium, dans une gamme

5 «Virtual Artist Studio Visit: Jinny Yu», YouTube < https://www.youtube.com/watch?v=4n33OcjDCls > à 3:15. (consulté le 25 novembre 2023)

6 Georgia O'Keeffe, *Untitled (Patio Door)*, ca. 1946, Graphite sur papier, 43,2 x 35.6 cm, Musée Georgia O'Keeffe, don de The Burnett Foundation, 1997.6.3 https://collections.okeeffemuseum.org/object/89

7 Voir Georgiana Uhlyarik, «The "Light One": A Case Study» dans *Georgia O'Keeffe* (Londres: Tate Publishing, 2016).

8 Anong Beam, pierres à peindre faites à la main à partir de matériaux récoltés sur l'île Manitoulin, en Ontario. https://www.beampaints.com/products/o-keeffe-and-martin-palettes?variant=39291853537349 (consulté le 25 novembre 2023) Palette d'[Agnès] Martin : Ultra Grey, Payne's Grey, Mars Black et Limestone White.

de bleus gris. Faisant tangentiellement référence aux bords et aux coins de sa série de 2018 intitulée *why does its lock fit my key?* et s'appuyant sur la possibilité du motif de la porte, ces nouvelles peintures introduisirent une forme centrale pliée – un cuboïde en devenir. Elles la préparèrent en douceur à l'explosion de couleurs qui survint lors de sa résidence d'un mois à La Napoule, dans le sud-est de la France, en avril 2022.

C'est dans un concours de circonstances pratiques, naturelles et artistiques que Yu a réalisé une série d'aquarelles lumineuses et colorées, intitulée plus tard *Inextricably Ours W* (2022). Un cuboïde bancal (*wonky cuboid*), comme elle l'appelle, était apparu et persistait dans son imagination depuis un certain temps. Depuis des mois, elle en avait fait des variantes sous forme de dessins au trait. Confiante qu'il y résidait un grand potentiel, Yu s'est saisie de l'extraordinaire qualité de la lumière de la côte méditerranéenne en s'autorisant à utiliser toute la gamme de couleurs du coffret d'aquarelles Holbein qu'elle avait emmené avec elle en raison de sa portabilité. Elle a passé ce mois à composer différentes permutations de ce cuboïde métamorphe. Parfois, ses facettes sont des tons différents d'une même couleur : orange, jaune, bleu. Dans d'autres, elles sont colorées de diverses teintes apparentées. Ses marques sont visibles, uniformes, et révèlent les couches et la méthode d'application. Les facettes sont translucides, mais aussi distinctes, ce qui confère à la forme un caractère à la fois éloigné et saillant. Les contours ne sont pas des lignes tracées, mais plutôt le résultat de la rencontre de facettes. La couleur environnante varie entre un contraste élevé avec l'image centrale – comme le vert et le jaune (*W22-05* P. 32) – et des changements subtils, parfois des oranges (*W22-01* P. 33) ou des bleus (*W22-02* P. 33).

Ces aquarelles dynamiques et fascinantes sont en constante évolution. En travaillant et en retravaillant les facettes, les couleurs, le motif des coups de pinceau et les compositions, Yu tente de résister à un rapport hiérarchique entre la figure et le fond. « J'ai eu l'idée d'aplanir la subordination hiérarchique », a-t-elle expliqué, cherchant à créer un espace partagé d'équilibre, d'être simplement en relation les uns avec les autres. Ses cuboïdes flottent dans un état intermédiaire de solidité suggérée et de perméabilité sans limites. Chacune suggère son propre état de devenir; considérées ensemble, elles créent un rythme synchronisé de formes et de couleurs rayonnantes, en mutation, interdépendantes et pourtant cohérentes.

De retour dans son atelier de peinture, Yu a commencé à explorer avec l'huile sur aluminium – le support qu'elle préconise depuis 2004 – les façons dont ses aquarelles avaient articulé de nouvelles directions picturales. *Inextricably Ours*

22-01, 2022 [P. 27], est un cuboïde à facettes orange, rouge et ocre dans un champ de vert recouvert de légères stries orange. Le vert à la fois rayonne et encercle le cuboïde, et s'interprète comme un plan autonome qui s'étend au-delà du bord du tableau. Les six arêtes de la forme délimitent la figure centrale et la placent en contraste complémentaire avec le vert. Les coups de pinceau de chaque facette sont visibles, vaporeux, superposés et laborieux, mais paraissent exécutés sans effort. Ils sont soigneusement organisés et orientés, ce qui implique une logique interne ou un système. Les facettes peuvent être lues séparément ou dans une variété de combinaisons – comme deux triangles adjacents peuvent se rejoindre perceptivement pour former un quadrilatère avec deux tonalités différentes, créant ainsi de la profondeur. Prise individuellement, la couleur uniforme de chaque facette souligne la planéité de sa forme. Ensemble, les couleurs créent un état d'entre-deux et de tout à la fois. Chaque facette dans l'image peut être distincte en termes de couleur ou de direction du trait, mais la composition se fond dans un tout, grâce à l'application uniforme du médium. Le cuboïde est une forme active, mais contenue, dont les bords ne sont jamais tout à fait nets, jamais clairement définis. Yu produit un jeu de formes géométriques qui se courbent vers l'intérieur et l'extérieur, puis se regroupent à nouveau. Dans chacune des peintures de cette période, il y a un intervalle où l'œil peut se reposer plus longtemps et se restaurer, avant que la direction des coups de pinceau ne reparte dans et autour de la composition.

Yu travaille sur plusieurs tableaux à la fois, ce qui permet de laisser sécher chaque couche avant d'appliquer la suivante. Ce processus est bien adapté à son projet continu, car il permet à de nouvelles idées de se greffer à des compositions antérieures. Dans cette série, la peinture recouvre toute la feuille de métal avec des degrés de translucidité variables, ce qui contrôle la réflectivité de l'aluminium dans la peinture. Dans une œuvre comme *Inextricably Ours 23-03*, 2023 [P. 44], l'aluminium s'infiltre à travers plusieurs facettes du cuboïde, en contraste avec l'opacité de la surface qui l'entoure. Dans les aquarelles de l'artiste, la lumière émane de l'intérieur, tandis que dans les huiles, la réflexion de la lumière environnante active la luminosité. Alors que certaines peintures font référence aux aquarelles et que d'autres sont des compositions nouvellement conçues, travailler à l'huile à une échelle beaucoup plus grande redéfinit la relation de la figure avec le fond.

Les peintures presque monochromes rouge cadmium de 2023 – *Inextricably Ours 23-02* [P. 29], *Inextricably Ours 23-03* [P. 44], et *Inextricably Ours 23-04* [P. 37] – confondent l'interrelation planaire entre le cuboïde et le plan. Tout en restant des espaces encore quelque peu délimités, ils sont réunis pour ne faire qu'un et être les deux à la fois. Esthétiquement généreuses et invitantes, ces compositions rouges sont autoreproductrices, répétitives et complètes, et en relation les unes avec les autres. Une nouvelle dimension apparaît dans *Inextricably Ours 23-04* P.37. Trois lignes, prenant naissance en un point du cuboïde, s'étendent au-delà de sa forme, atteignant le bord de la feuille d'aluminium, l'une d'entre elles rencontrant le coin inférieur gauche du tableau. Ces extensions produisent une échelle différente et revendiquent l'espace au-delà du tableau lui-même comme faisant partie intégrante de la composition. Les lignes se connectent de multiples façons les unes aux autres et produisent plusieurs interrelations. Le rouge se décline en plusieurs nuances. Les formes apparaissent, se dissolvent et subsistent, se relayant patiemment à tour de rôle. Elles s'étendent vers le haut et vers l'extérieur, vers l'intérieur et vers le bas. Ce n'est pas que la composition soit instable, mais plutôt qu'elle se métamorphose en permanence, marquant le début de l'ouverture du cuboïde. Yu part de cette limite sans prédétermination, « pour voir ce qui se passe » et pour ouvrir des possibilités au lieu de les fermer.

Travaillant dans son studio berlinois au début de l'année 2023, Yu a expérimenté les gouaches Caran d'Ache pour ouvrir les cuboïdes dans ce médium matériellement séduisant et velouté. Dans sa série *Inextricably Ours* G de 2023, elle expérimente en étendant les plans de couleur vers les bords du papier, ce qui permet de les amplifier tout en ouvrant de nouvelles dimensions. N'étant plus contenues, ces compositions apparaissent moins stables, comme si elles étaient en train de muter.

Elles sont d'une myriade de couleurs – vert, bleu, jaune, rouge, orange, violet – créant une variété de rectangles et de polygones interdépendants. Vus ensemble, les plans de couleur s'étendent d'une feuille à l'autre, se combinant en composition dans l'espace de l'observateur.

Inextricably Ours 23-04 P.37 a été retravaillé à partir d'un état antérieur à la suite des dessins à la gouache. De retour dans son atelier de peinture à Ottawa, Yu a commencé à explorer cette approche dans une nouvelle série de peintures, tout en poursuivant celles qu'elle n'avait pas encore terminées. *Inextricably Ours 23-05* P.35, *Inextricably Ours 23-06* P.38, *Inextricably Ours 23-07* P.34, et *Inextricably Ours 23-08* P.39 sont conçues de cette manière – les plans ne sont plus prévisibles, l'échelle n'est plus perceptible, mais intuitive, les couleurs sont abondantes. Ces images puissantes se présentent sans référent ni hiérarchie interne, créant et recréant des interrelations, négociant et partageant leur espace à la fois en tant qu'hôtes et invités.

Le travail d'atelier est un travail d'imagination. La pratique picturale de Jinny Yu est captivante par sa subtilité et sa retenue. Profondément philosophique, son travail est poétiquement politique et discrètement beau. Comme tous les artistes engagés, Yu puise dans la plénitude du monde qui l'entoure, ce qui résonne avec le plus de pertinence pour elle, et transforme un geste, un matériau, une image ou une pensée en un voyage immersif dans sa conscience, son état d'esprit. Elle nous invite à entrer dans ses fragments de pensée alors qu'ils se révèlent petit à petit et tout à la fois – à toujours ralentir et à méditer sur des contradictions suspendues de manière éthérée, non pas pour être résolues, mais plutôt absorbées. Sa capacité à analyser des distinctions fines et poignantes révèle qu'elle est très à l'écoute des dynamiques de pouvoir et qu'elle possède une fibre sensible et réceptive à travers laquelle elle comprend et perçoit les choses. ■

↓ Left to right | Gauche à droite
Hôte I – Hôte XLII, 2020
graphite on paper | graphite sur papier
42 × 42 cm each | chaque
Montreal Museum of Fine Arts Collection |
Collection du Musée des beaux-arts
de Montréal

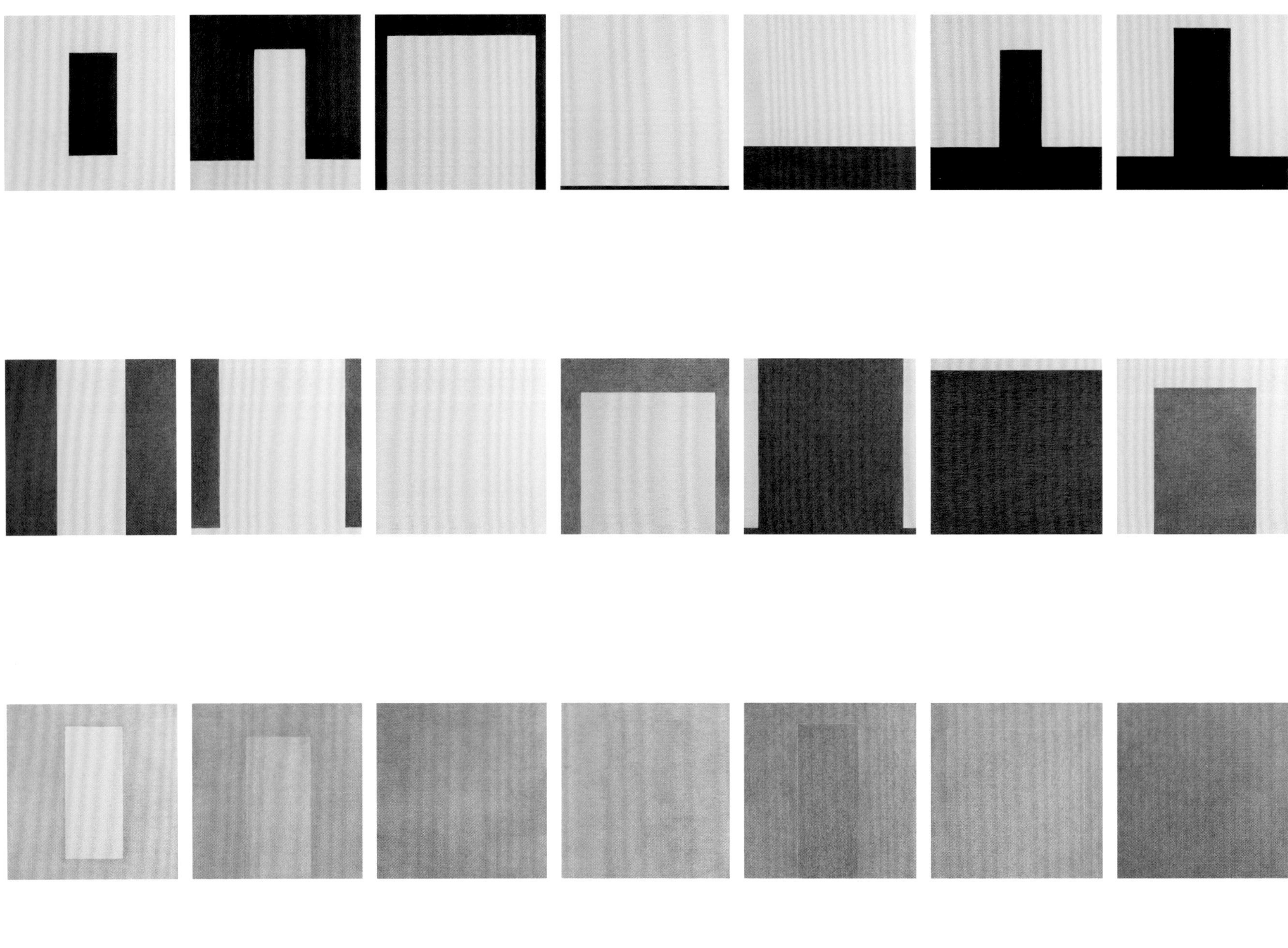

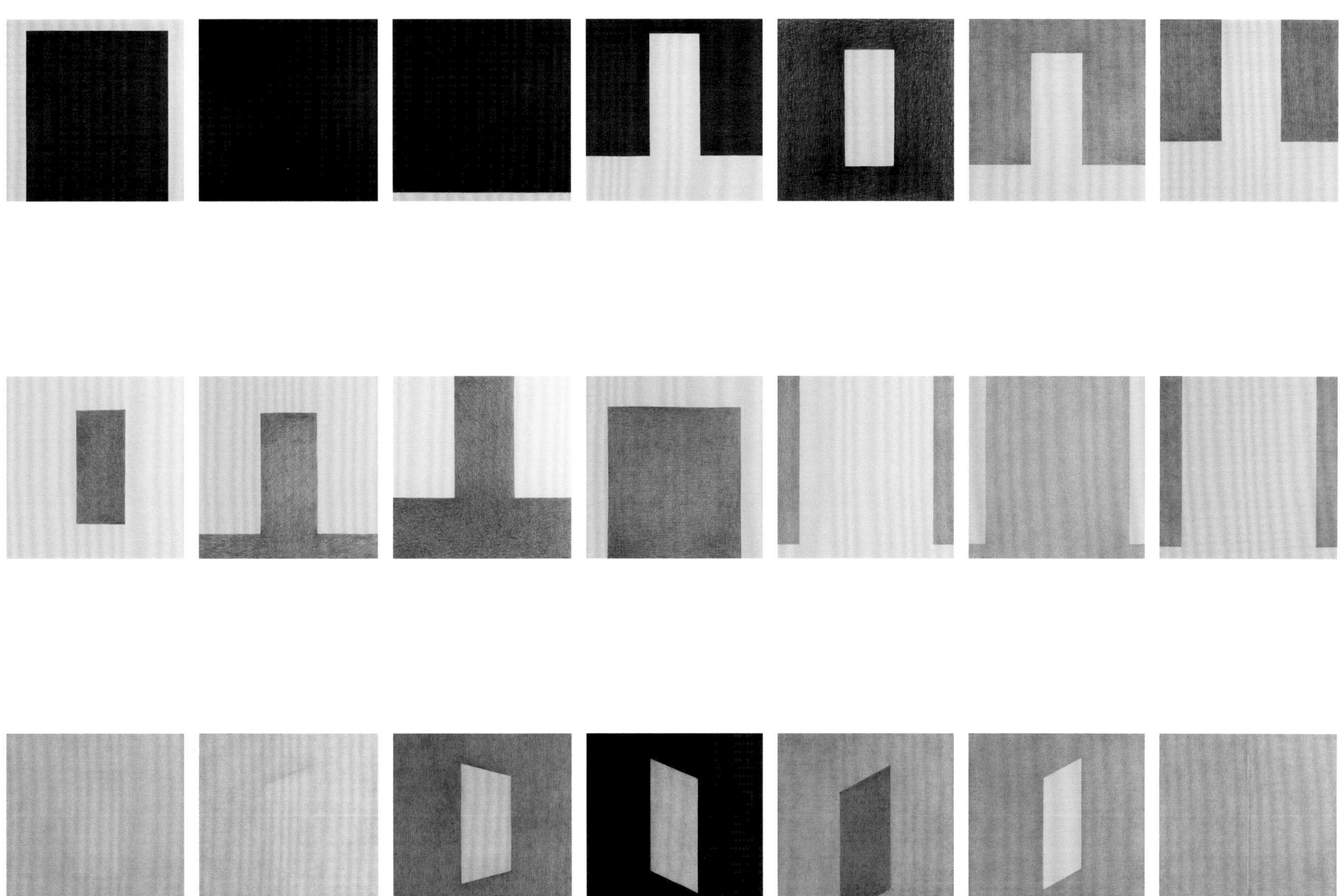

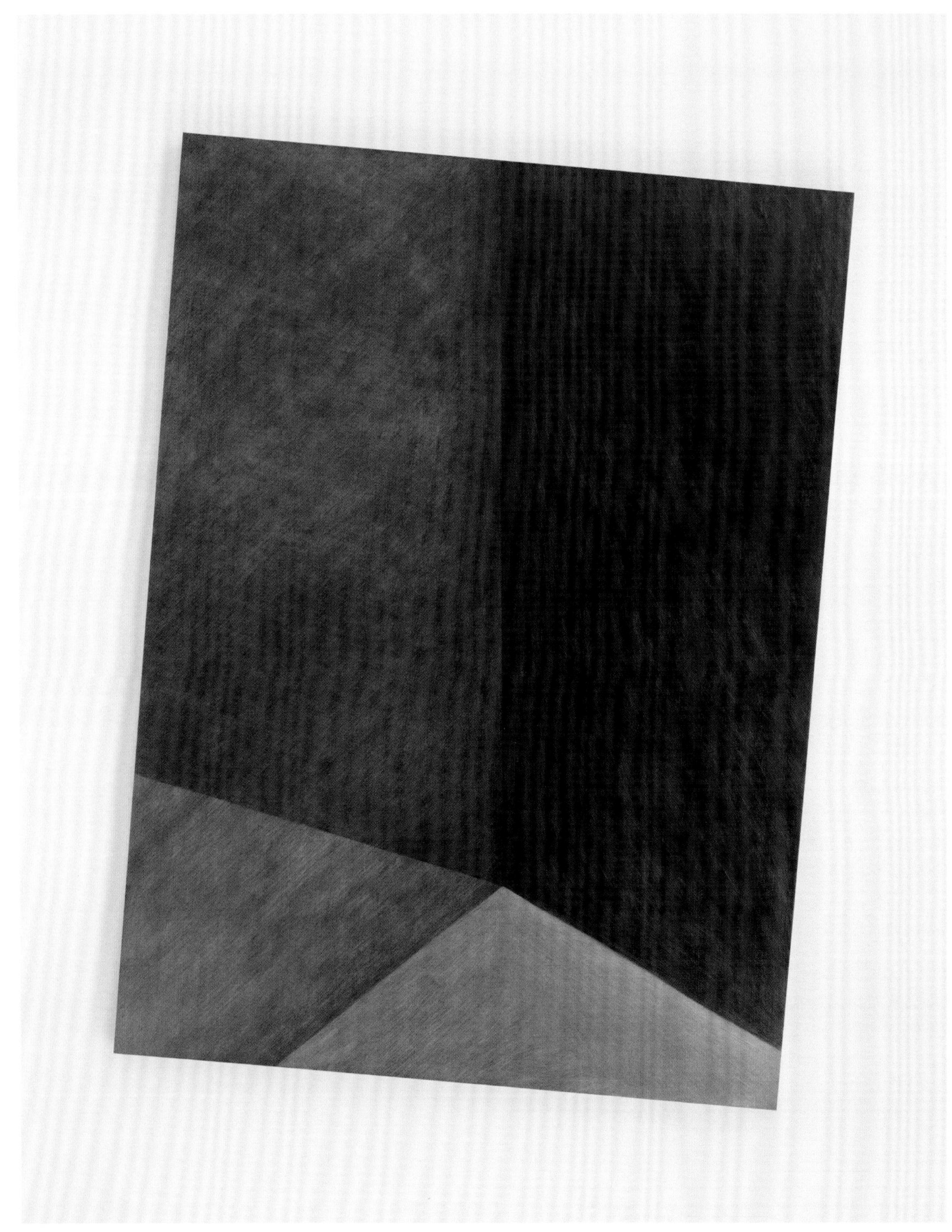

←*why does its lock fit my key?*, 2018
oil on aluminium | huile sur aluminium
130 × 102 cm

→*why does its lock fit my key?*, 2018
oil on aluminium | huile sur aluminium
147 × 116 cm

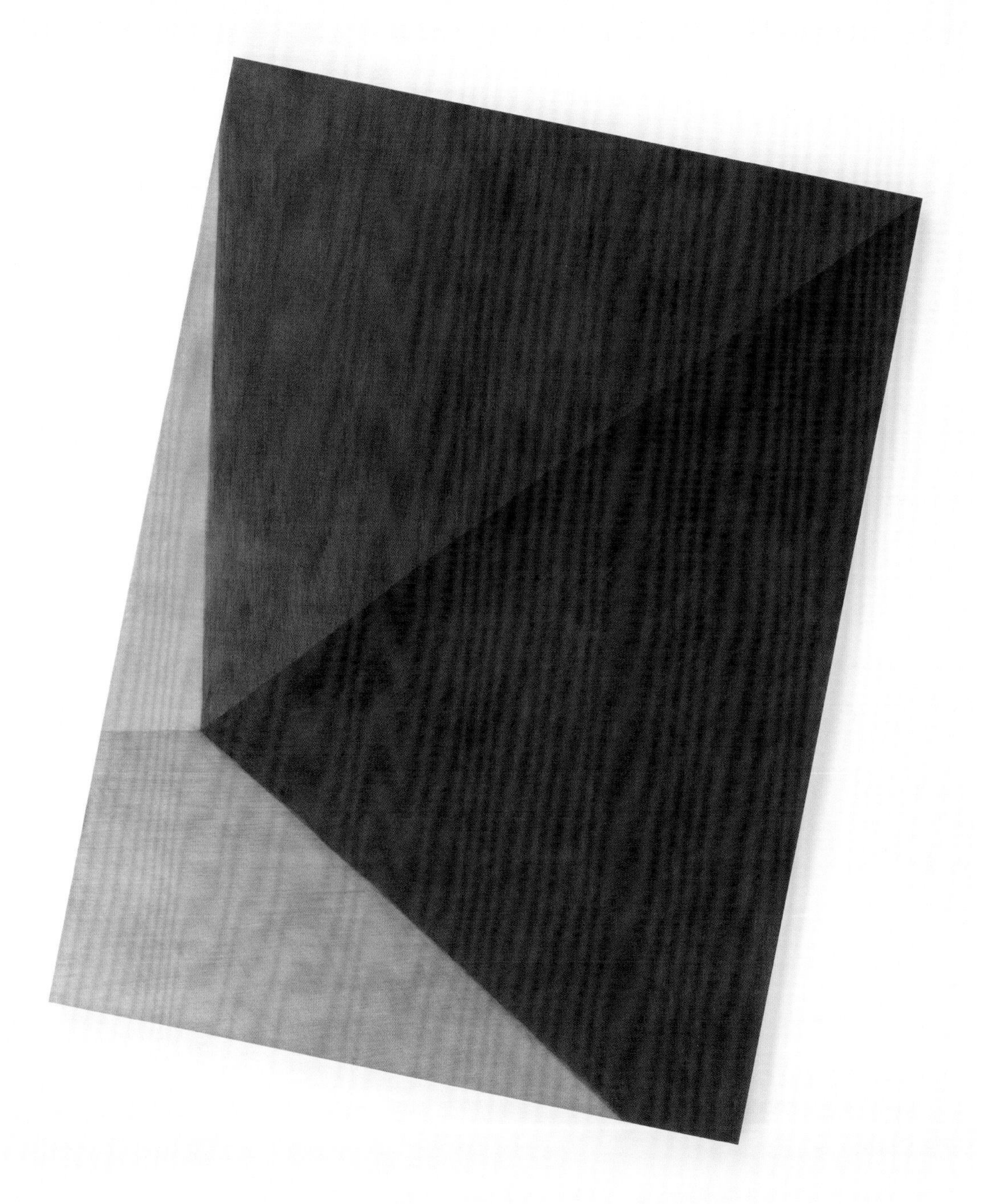

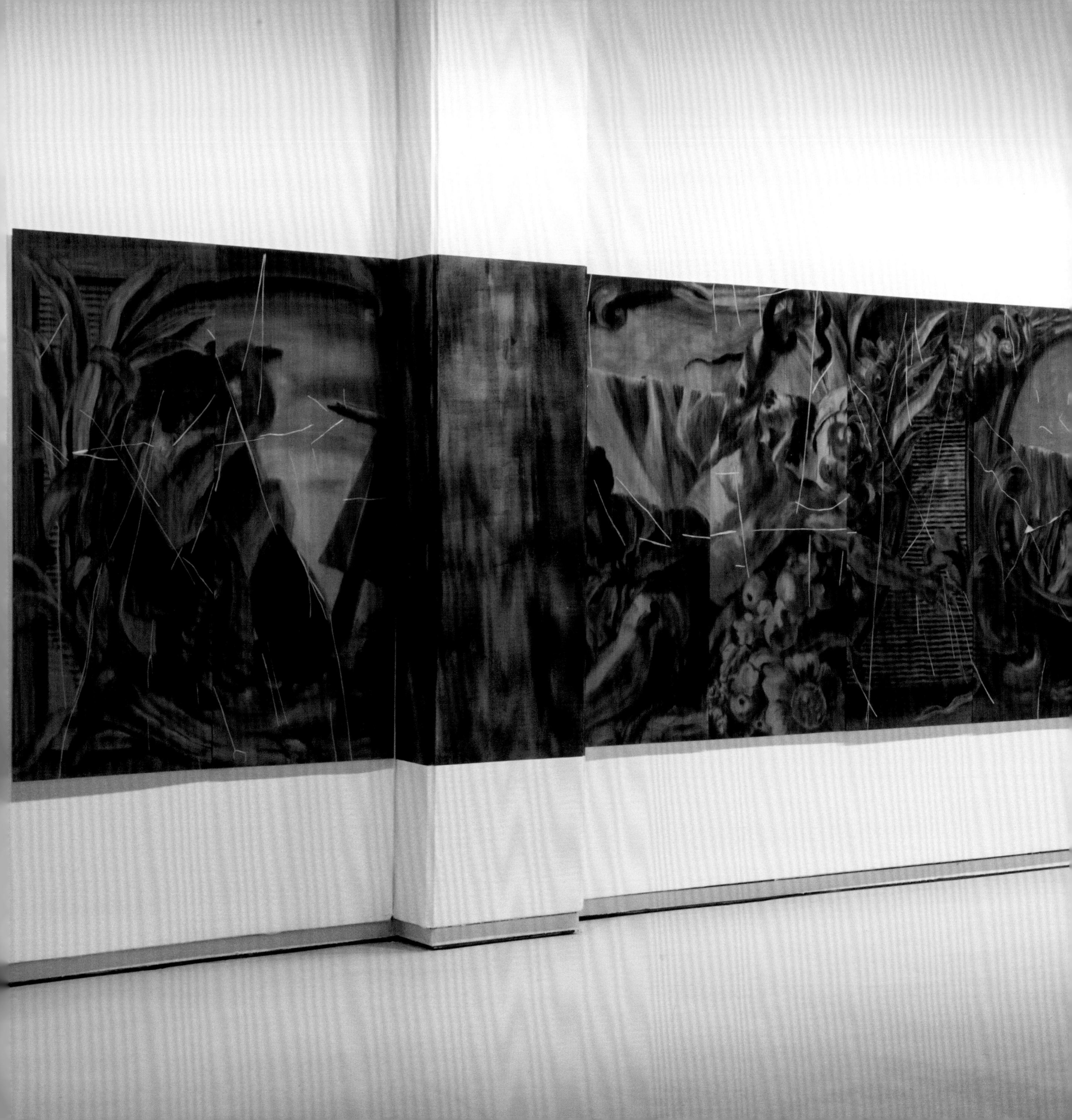

Becoming in Place

Patrick Flores

Devenir en place

Patrick Flores

Tiepolo Project, 2011
oil on aluminum | huile sur aluminium
164 × 1341 × 483 cm
Installation view, *Cadenza*
March 23 – May 26, 2013 |
23 mars – 26 mars 2013
St. Mary's University Art Gallery, Halifax
Confederation Centre Art Gallery Collection |
Collection du Musée d'art du Centre
de la Confédération, Charlottetown

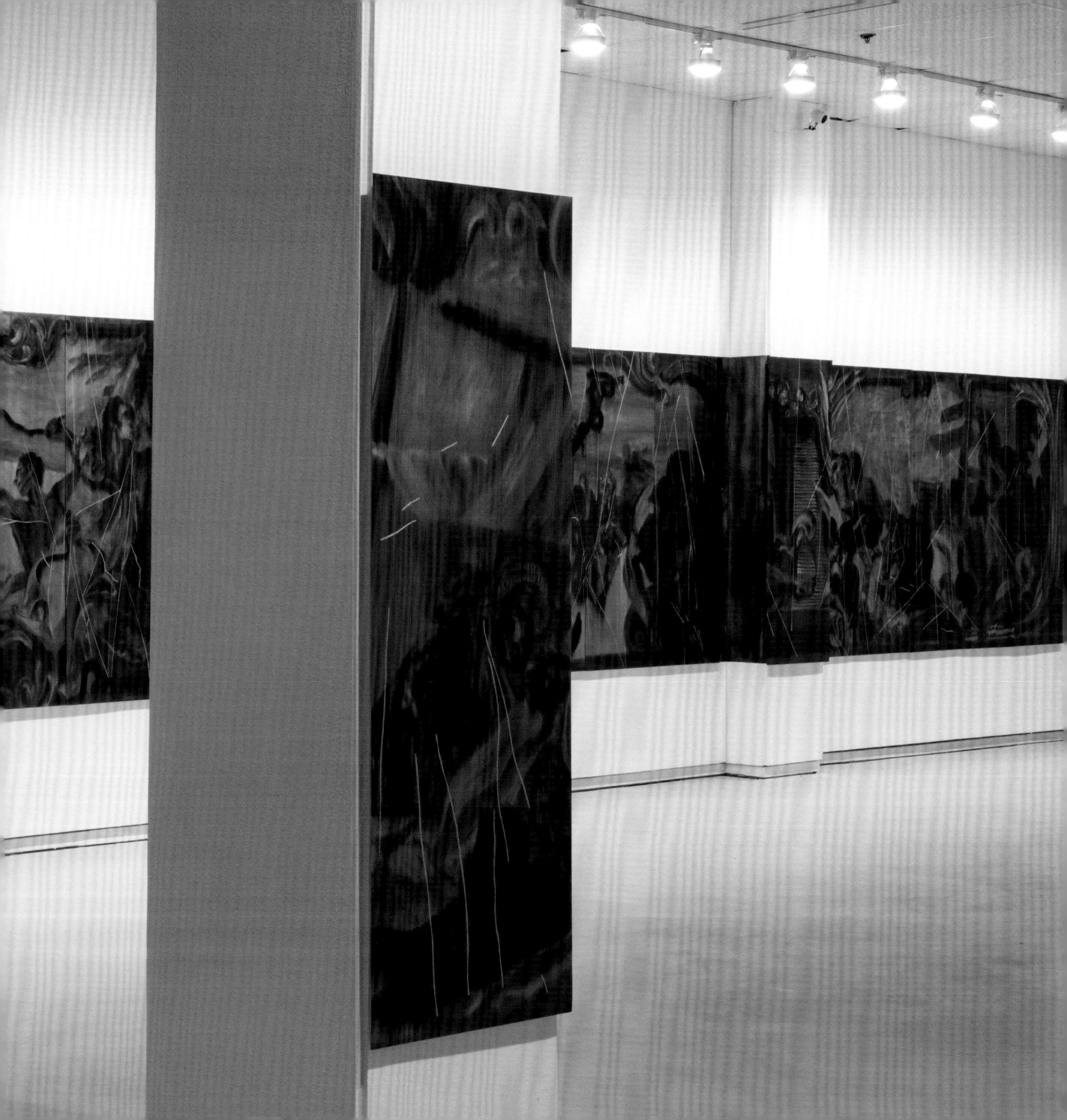

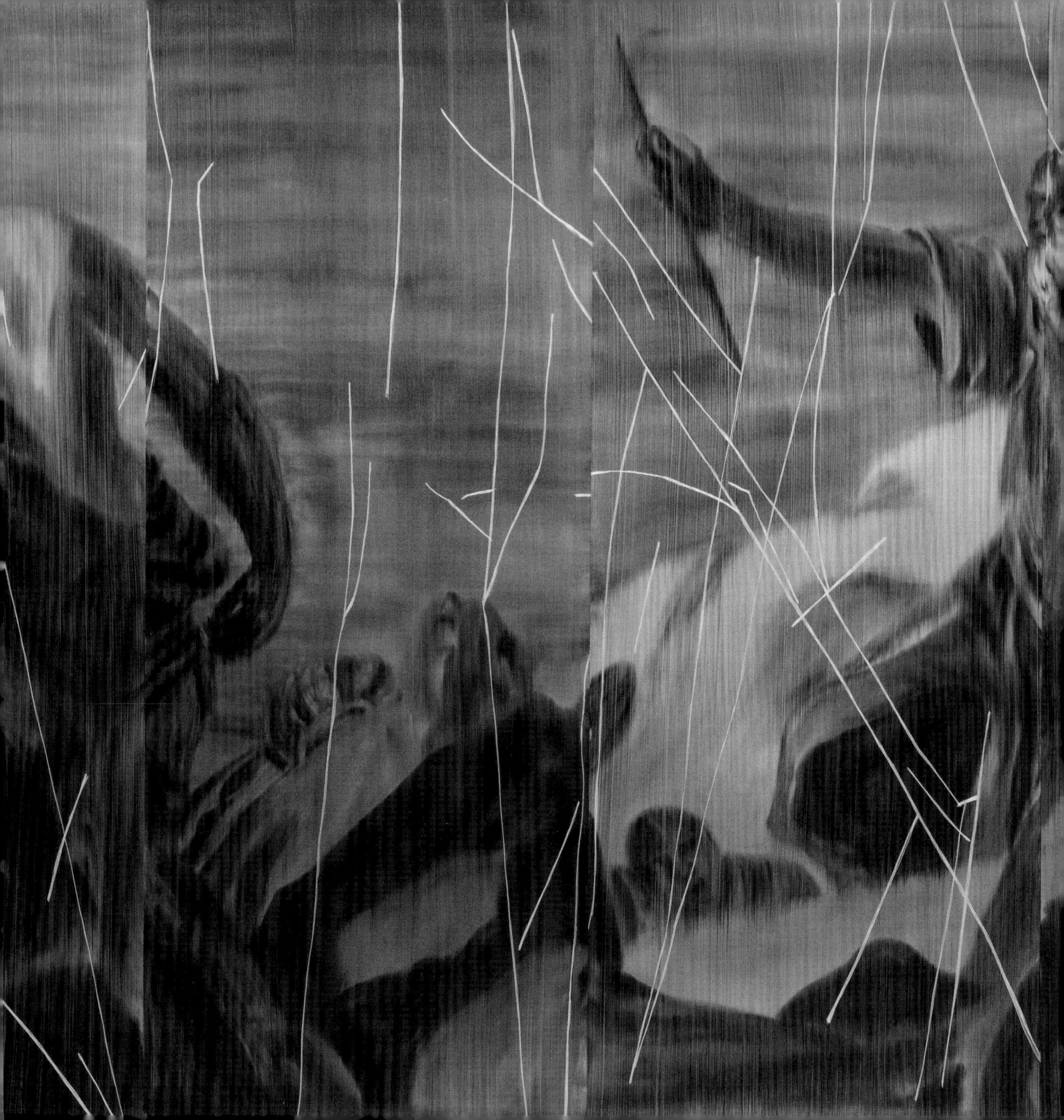

The instinct for the art-world rubric of abstraction elaborates on the promise of openness, particularly of resisting what a well-known artist calls the "dead weight of the real world." This real world, however, also hones this wide-eyed instinct that is often reduced to the medium-specificity of the "abstract." Surely, the promise of openness, the resistance of the instinct, and the habits of institutional recognition need not bind abstraction to whichever fixed point proves convenient for either the shorthand of naming or the capture of interpretation. There ought to arise across these coordinates of generative tension a moment of reprieve for the abstract to be able to emerge at the limit.

Tiepolo Project (detail | détail), 2011
oil on aluminum | huile sur aluminium
164 × 1341 × 483 cm
Confederation Centre Art Gallery Collection | Collection du Musée d'art du Centre de la Confédération, Charlottetown

Jinny Yu has been confronting this condition of interrogation: to seek the light that sheds on how form can be arrested from drifting towards a terminus, or a preconceived prophecy. Instead, that same light may be envisioned to facet the angle of limit through which the incipience of the instinct finds the chance to become particular, because it is precisely abstract; its material not a dead weight, but the real world itself of another realm.

Part of this limit is sensing the inchoate form that Yu coaxes from the welter of her inspirations as well as the urgencies of the surrounding society. And so, as a student of her art, I will also try another way to write with and through her, alongside another artist whom she met while at art school in Montréal. This artist is Lani Maestro (b. 1957), a Filipino who migrated to Canada in the 1980s. As I share a part of Maestro's cultural subjectivity, so does she form part of Yu's trajectory as an artist. Through Maestro's own text and my response to it, an essay on abstraction may configure in relation to the propositions of Yu's œuvre through the years.

According to Yu:

"I met Lani in the late '90s during my undergraduate studies at Concordia University in Montréal. Lani and her then partner had invited me and my friend, who was completing his master's degree in film production at the same

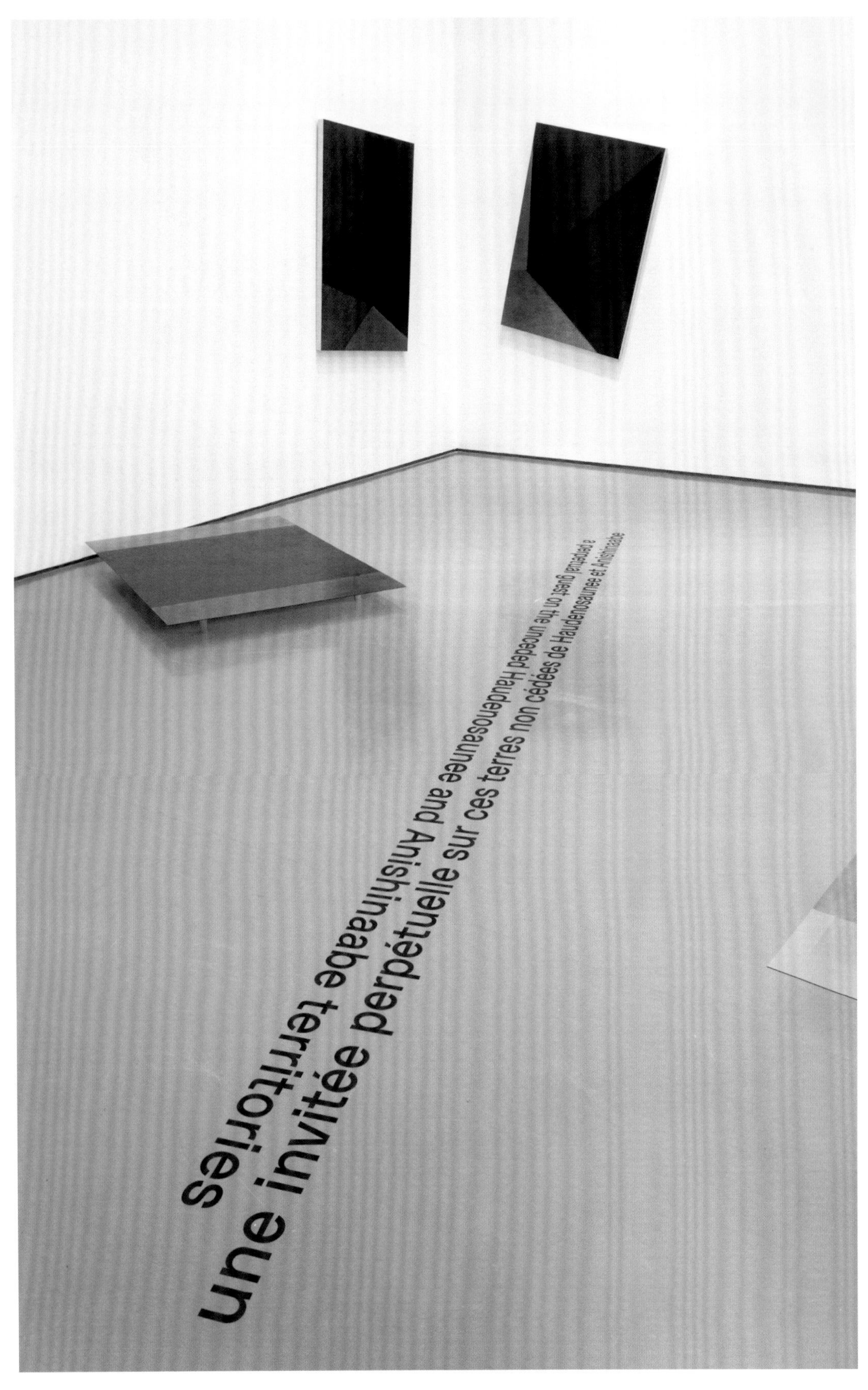

why does its lock fit my key?, 2018
oil on aluminium | huile sur aluminium
130 × 102 cm, 147 × 116 cm
and | et
Perpetual Guest, 2019
Oil on glass and aluminium pilons |
huile sur vitre et pilons d'aluminium
10 × 152 × 102 cm

Installation view | vue d'installation,
RELATIONS: Diaspora and Painting |
RELATIONS: la diaspora et la peinture
July 8 - November 29, 2020 |
8 juillet – 29 novembre 2020
PHI Foundation for Contemporary Art |
Fondation PHI pour l'art contemporain,
Montréal

> university, to their home in the Plateau. If I recall correctly, Lani was a professor in one of his courses. I was surprised that a professor would invite a student and his friend to her home and felt honoured to be welcomed. Her cozy home was in one of those typical Plateau duplexes. We entered her living room from the frozen streets of Montréal and sat on her sofa talking, snacking, and drinking. I don't remember much of what was said, but I remember her as a most generous person and graceful host. My friend, whose English was limited as he had recently moved from South Korea via France, often talked about how generous she was as a professor and mentor. We both thought she would be a good role model for us, particularly as she was the only non-white professor with whom we had interacted till then. My contact with her was limited to the couple of visits, but of the short times I had spent at her house, I felt welcomed, warm and comfortable."[1]

This vignette of contact and encounter between two artists of migrant heritage is vital in creating the atmosphere of abstraction as an atmosphere of openness, a hospitality that dissipates a harsh winter or the density of a foreign language. When I told Maestro about Yu, she struggled to remember, but she would confirm the shared sentiment and the mutual experience of working through an at once fuzzy and resettled subjectivity:

> what she recounted is true as i tried to welcome the foreign students especially those who did not speak english very well. also, there was a split between the french and the english and i did my best to address that 'divide'. in those days, the discussions around identity politics, i.e. race, gender was interesting. also, troubling and exciting for both students and faculty. i felt the empowerment from students who gained confidence in their explorations of 'self'. i learned a lot from this exchange and worked hard to arrive at a position less divisive, less ideological . . . and always made artworks, the priority in their exploration of their subjectivities.[2]

These recollections from Yu and Maestro are annotations of practice and inform a possible reflection on abstraction in history and as a way of making things and interacting with persons. In other words, the subjectivity that is so at stake

1 Email correspondence with the author, July 14, 2023.
2 Email correspondence with the author, July 30, 2023. The quotation preserves Maestro's original capitalization.

in the work of the artist is the materiality of the form itself, the agency of its sensuousness. The challenge is how to convey these energies into a certain textual exercise. Primordial in this regard is Yu's exploration of the abstract form. It mainly consists of slates that are delicately inscribed, or better still, smeared or stained with pigment or graphite, though sometimes swarmed, too, by frantic markings as if they were voyaging starlings. To be gleaned in this procedure is the desire to overcome binary fields like voids and enclosures, or positive and negative spaces, impressions of dimension or ciphers of abyss. The artist instead strives for an alternation or the adjacency of tone and angle, edge and gesture, fold and convergence, and overlaps to yield networks, vibrations or resonances, and even ornaments. In one instance, paint on transparent glass is suspended, but is proximate to the concrete floor, separated by aluminum. Yu's geometry, though disciplined, is liberal in its ventures into decisive chromatic variations, permutations of potential dwelling, gradations of her hand's pressure, or how light leaks from a slit of faint, yet adamant, lines, both sinuous and quietly hectic. Here and there, a semblance of a portal pulsates, either advancing or receding within an ashen cosmos, or a polemical text challenges the comfortable intelligence. If one were tempted to name the apparitions, they might be rooms or furniture or manifesto, familiar but never banal. Eventually, this grammar of abstraction dilates into installation, widening the latitude as well as the potential feeling of the erstwhile painting.

The meeting between Yu and Maestro would foreshadow the former's desire for the installative attitude. It happened in a loft that Maestro built for gatherings in a complex that housed an artistic community. The loft is a curious space, usually cantilevered, suspended as in a bridge but still holding volume as it floats. In many ways it is what Derrida might call a supplement, something that is not added to further expand the existing structure, or extract a core, but which pursues another path to create another vicinity and assemble people, bringing to light or exposing the lack that does not need so much to be filled as to be the beginning of another relationality that addresses, and hopefully overcomes, though does not belabour, otherness or identity.

In many ways, such labour of abstraction is an ethos of belonging, a constant effort to stake out both boundary and beginning. As Yu introspects: "The sense of belonging, I find, often leads to a stronger sense of responsibility. Would a settler, for example, who truly belongs and cares, exercise responsibility towards the land together with Indigenous peoples, and not only extract resources from

Tiepolo Project (detail | détail), 2011
oil on aluminum | huile sur aluminium
164 × 1341 × 483 cm
Confederation Centre Art Gallery Collection |
Collection du Musée d'art du Centre
de la Confédération, Charlottetown

Installation view | vue d'installation
Cadenza, March 23 – May 26, 2013 |
23 mars – 26 mai 2013
St. Mary's University Art Gallery, Halifax

it? Or would a proper sense of respect from a guest be better/enough? Should a Perpetual Guest adopt a sense of belonging?"[3]

The promise of this belonging may well be the fulfillment of a political intuition, though the passage may have begun from an uncanny site. It is a spiritual locus, specifically Catholic. Her experience of living in Venice between 2005 and 2016, immersing herself within an architecture of paintings and intense daily devotion to images, stayed with her to the extent that it led her "to reject the idea that painting is autonomous, contained only within its four corners. I realized that painting has to interact with, and is always affected by, the space it is in."[4] This anxiety is further fleshed out when she closely reads the aging of the work of Tiepolo (b. 1696) in which it is through the index of time, in the manner of material attrition, that a space opens up the modernist enterprise to essential precarity, one that is laid bare as having a Christian genealogy as well as a postcolonial afterlife of repossession.

In an account of her engagement with Tiepolo's *Brazen Serpent* (1731–1732), a painting of judgment and punishment, she explicates how the piece achieves contemporaneity when it is unhinged from the fantasy of autonomy:

> It was rather the cracks and striations that were the most important for me in this painting. When I saw it here at the Accademia Gallery in 2008, I was thinking about the relationship between illusional and actual space, and the materiality of paint. The striation is basically void of paint, so it is physically further away from the viewer (however microscopic it is) compared to the surface of the painting, which is describing an illusional space. The fact that the striation that is physically further from us is visually closer to us, and that the painted surface that is physically close to us is actually representing a space beyond that surface, is what interested me. Basically, to me, that painting by Tiepolo was the contemporary painting.[5]

That Yu discerns a fluid lacuna internally, or intrinsically, and in doing so widens the ambit of abstraction, can only be traced to her attentiveness to the semiosis and socius that coalesce along with thinking abstractly, doing abstraction, and being hospitable to the ambience of the work, the sound and wind, for instance,

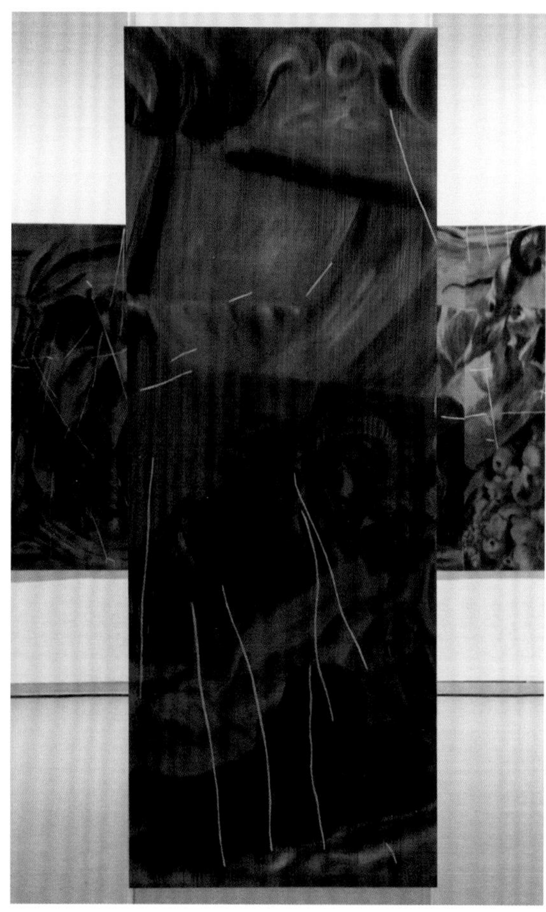

3 *entretiens # 3: conversation between amy fung, david garneau and jinny yu on perpetual guest* (Gatineau: Galerie UQO, 2019), 24.

4 *Jinny Yu: To Activate Space* (Montréal, Québec: Éditions Art Mûr, 2014), 35.

5 Ibid, 38.

which are the very contingencies rendering art charged and attuned, cogently present among the forces around it.

Beyond the formalism of abstraction, therefore, is its phenomenology, sharply evoked by the sensorium afforded by the artist's mindfulness of aluminum as a medium that takes in the environment and yet tends to resist the gravity of paint and the bureaucracy of painting, which is not totally assimilated by a metallic surface that may fully overdetermine the visual field with recognizable figuration, or image, or certain identities of both art and its practitioner. We are reminded here of how the abstractionist Suzan Frecon (b. 1941) would also be distracted, absorbed, almost bewitched by the Medieval Sienese painter Duccio's luminous painting *Madonna and Child* (c. 1290–1300): "It takes me out of myself... I get lost in it," regarding the painting as "always in a state of suspension."[6]

According to the critic and theorist Richard Shiff, this suspension is the interval between ecology and consciousness, the memory of forming: "Offsetting the unseen mathematical foundation, her visible surface is organic and irregular, as if she were working against herself... To this quirky geometry, she adds the active vibrations of hand rendering. Her paint, especially along ellipsoidal contours, develops an uneven appearance... Her composition... may well be experienced as anticomposition."[7] Frecon looks at this elusiveness as deriving from an impossibility: "It is impossible to say we aren't from nature."[8]

Maestro's early sorties into painting were abstractions, which she likens to weaving in their poignant, purposive intricacy and the persistence of vulnerable matrices which, like Yu's own granular meshes, enable light to slightly filter, or at least register an ember, or allude to water, or some kind of precipitation. From these paintings, she became more thoughtful and sensitive to the reminiscence, or the membrane, of lines. Consider how she describes her work *Sing Mother (Twilight eats you)*:

> sing mother (twilight eats you) is a series of drawings in ink that came about after a visit to korea a few years ago. in 2004, i went to see the dmz, the demilitarized zone that lines the border between the south and the north. i wanted to sense something of my father's history as a military officer who fought in the korean war in 1952. from where i stood, an air of abandonment wrapped

6 Suzan Frecon, "Suspension," in Richard Shiff, *Writing after Art: Essays on Modern and Contemporary Artists* (New York: David Zwirner Books, 2023), 199.

7 Ibid, 203.

8 Ibid.

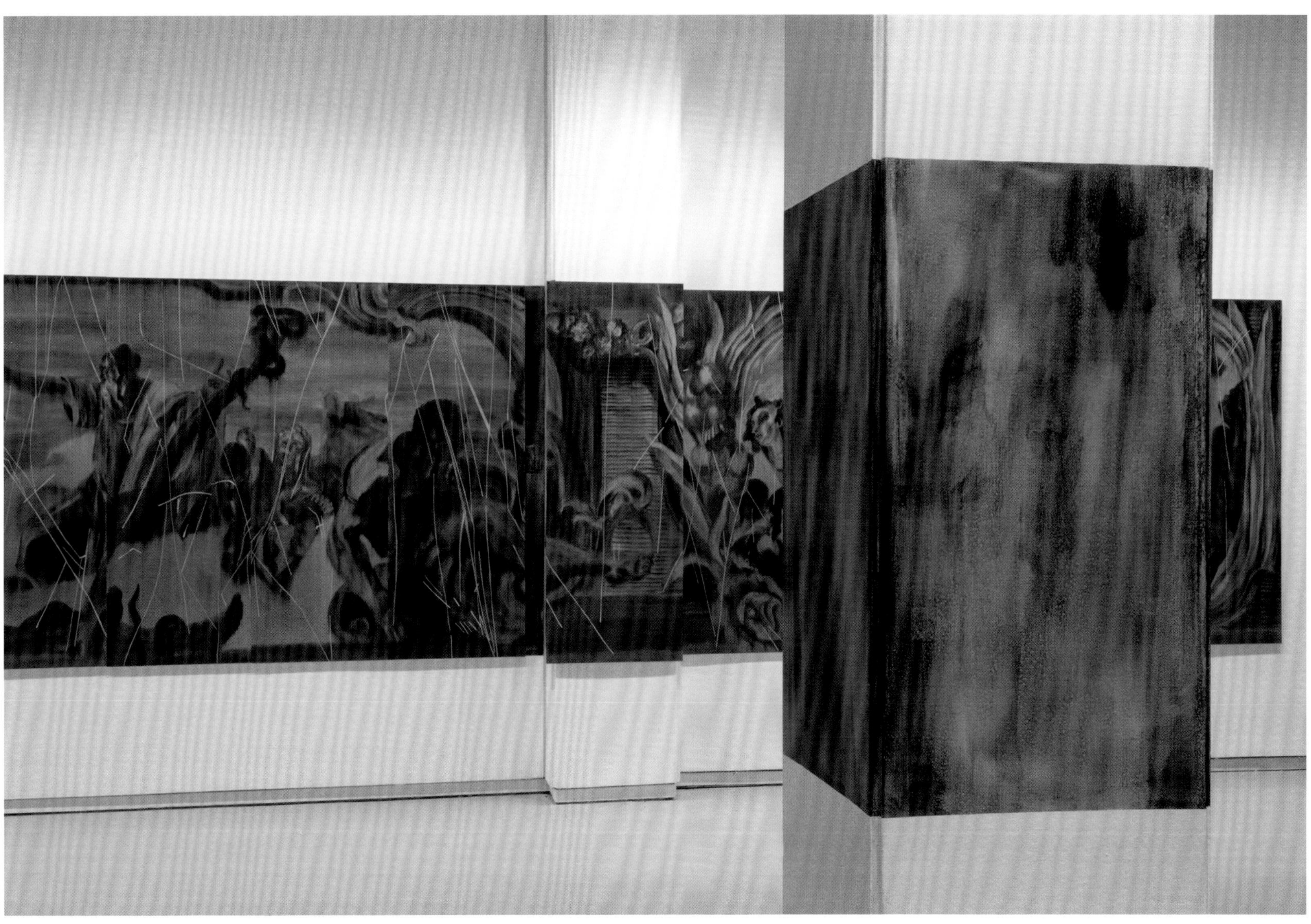

Tiepolo Project (detail | détail), 2011
oil on aluminum | huile sur aluminium
164 × 1341 × 483 cm
Confederation Centre Art Gallery Collection | Collection du Musée d'art du Centre de la Confédération, Charlottetown

Installation view | vue d'installation
Cadenza, March 23 – May 26, 2013 | 23 mars – 26 mai 2013
St. Mary's University Art Gallery, Halifax

> itself around this restricted, barren and menacing mined land brazed with miles of double fenced barbed wires and armed guards. an interesting phenomenon has arisen as this long strip of land has become a site of reflection for the politics that keep this country divided. it has become a sanctuary for rare species of sentient life.
>
> this liminal space became a place of refuge as i could not retrieve any kind of connection to the museological representations of war in the museum. i began drawing with an attempt to re-paint my mother's series of flower paintings and the work evolved into these series of 'drawings of abandon.' as some earlier works, sing mother commences from a narrative of some kind but the story escapes telling as it allows for other subjectivities to unravel... i find this 'betrayal' in language as something positive in the retrieval of self/ves as it makes the experience of otherness, of not knowing, much more apparent, more felt. it also poses the inadequacy of representation of reality as we experience it. i find that the liminal space of knowing and unknowing is an abstraction that we often arrive at if we are to remain open to the complexity of world as event. the regime of representation that marks our apprehension of history is what and where my work seems to often go to and unconsciously address — that throbbing line/space that marks experience and the language that evolves to make what we call 'memory.'
>
> words have always been present in my work as drawings, lines, thoughts, or invisible sources of inspiration. often, it is within the crevices of miscommunication, attempts to create a link with another, human or non-human, that i find the sensual existence of poetry.[9]

Yu's recent works involving oil paint on aluminum panels, and gouache and watercolour on paper, continue the delicacy with which she has deployed the vocabulary of abstraction. The algorithm of interacting shapes and shifting rectilinear matrices speaks to her investigations into the ties between host and guest within a migrant situation, the reciprocal, though fraught, toil underlying difficult generosities amid systemic racism and profound friendships and kindness. Modernism's neurosis about flatness finds a counterpoint, as in a polyphony, in the artist's intimations of rondure and investment in rhythm. The layers of thin

9 Lani Maestro, letter to Susan Gibson Garvey, 2006, courtesy of Lani Maestro.

glazes, laid out ostensibly with remarkable discipline, evince a certain gleam or sheen, even as the lyrical polychrome is ascendant and tends to mesmerize. Such a transparency that is also an iridescence may hearken back to a childhood of toys or even a table laden with gelatin for dessert!

This insistence and patience with inscription on surfaces fundamentally sustain the complex politics of being current and salient in a world that excludes, discriminates, and alienates and in an art that, like the "brazen gestures" in the nascent abstraction of Maestro, is able to intimate the impossibility of presence, or the disavowal of content that is prone to be instrumentalized. That said, the woman artist who engages with abstraction also performs the theatre of visibility, of the fraught tactic of representation as she invites "wind, sky, and rain."[10] If abstraction were ultimately non-objective, it is because the woman artist is the medium of the subjective.

Both Yu and Maestro pursue the joy of this sensual existence even as they hover around the trouble of the "other," the "structure," the "nature." At once, joy and trouble incite and inspire to conceive of the rightful abstraction in which they — women and migrants and artists — can truthfully live. ◆

10 Lani Maestro in email correspondence with the author, October 10, 2023.

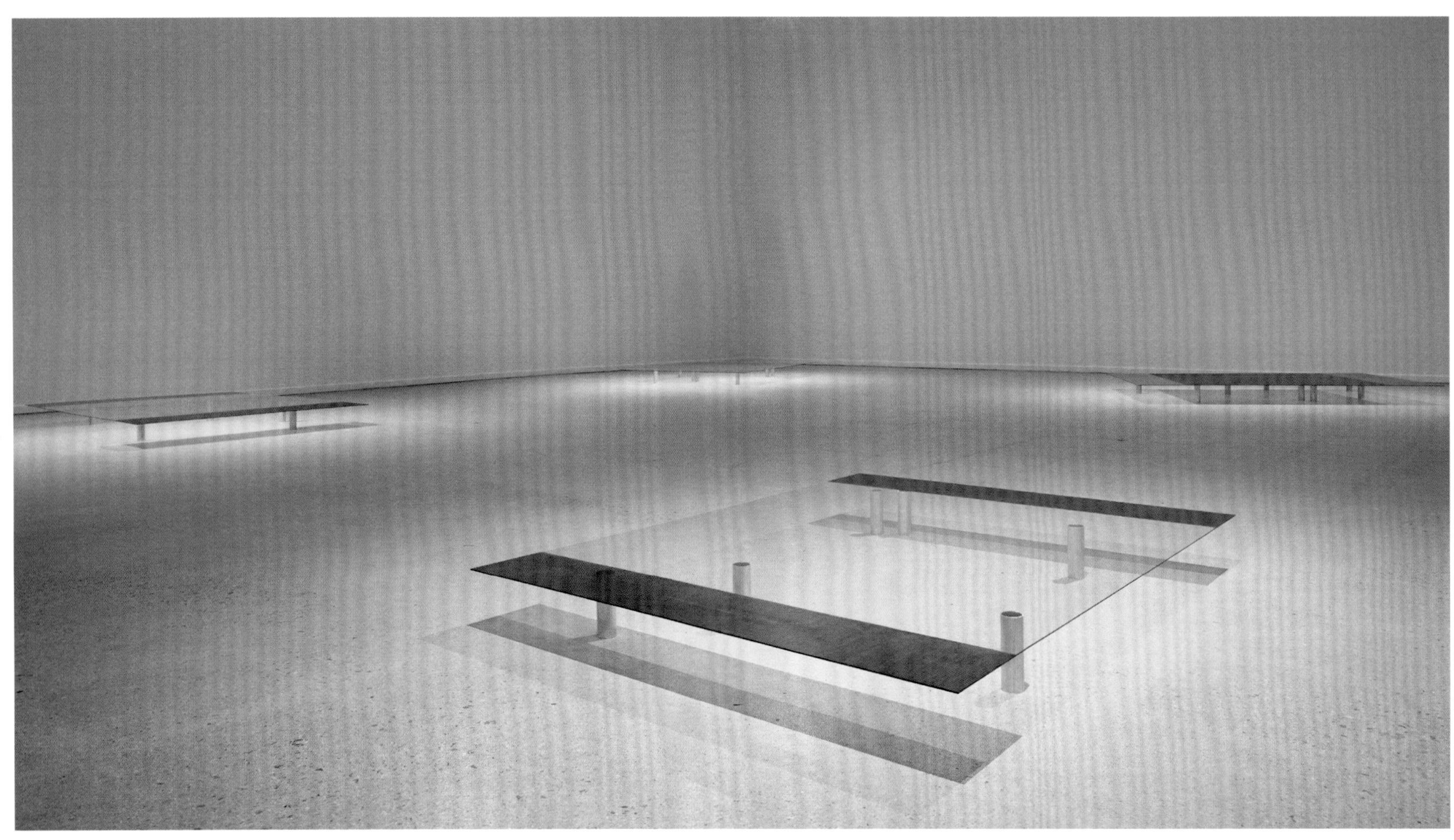

Installation view | vue d'installation
Perpetual Guest
November 6 – December 7, 2019 |
6 novembre – 7 décembre 2019
Galerie UQO, Gatineau

Perpetual Guest, 2019
oil on glass and aluminium pilons |
huile sur vitre et pilons d'aluminium
10 × 152 × 102 cm

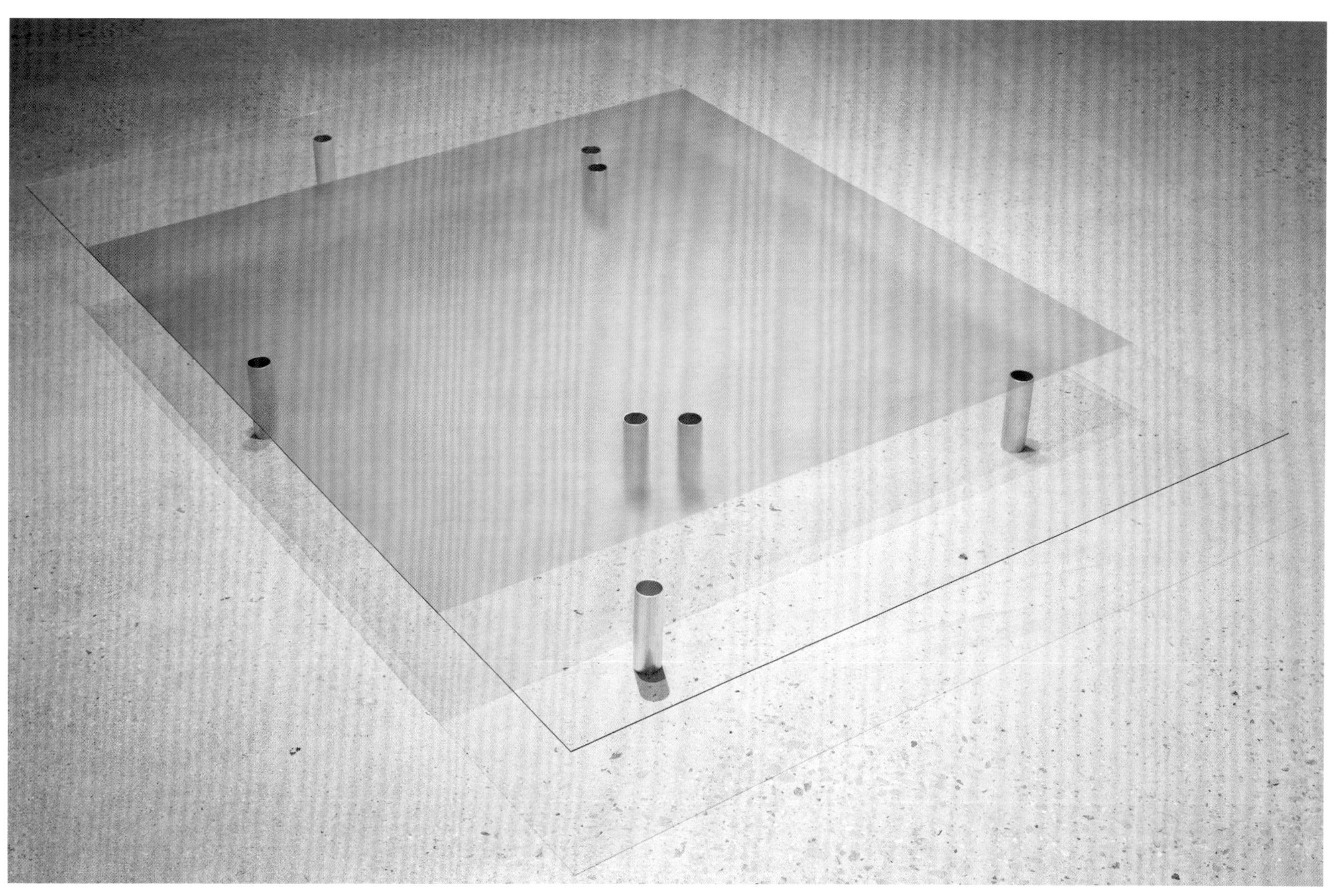

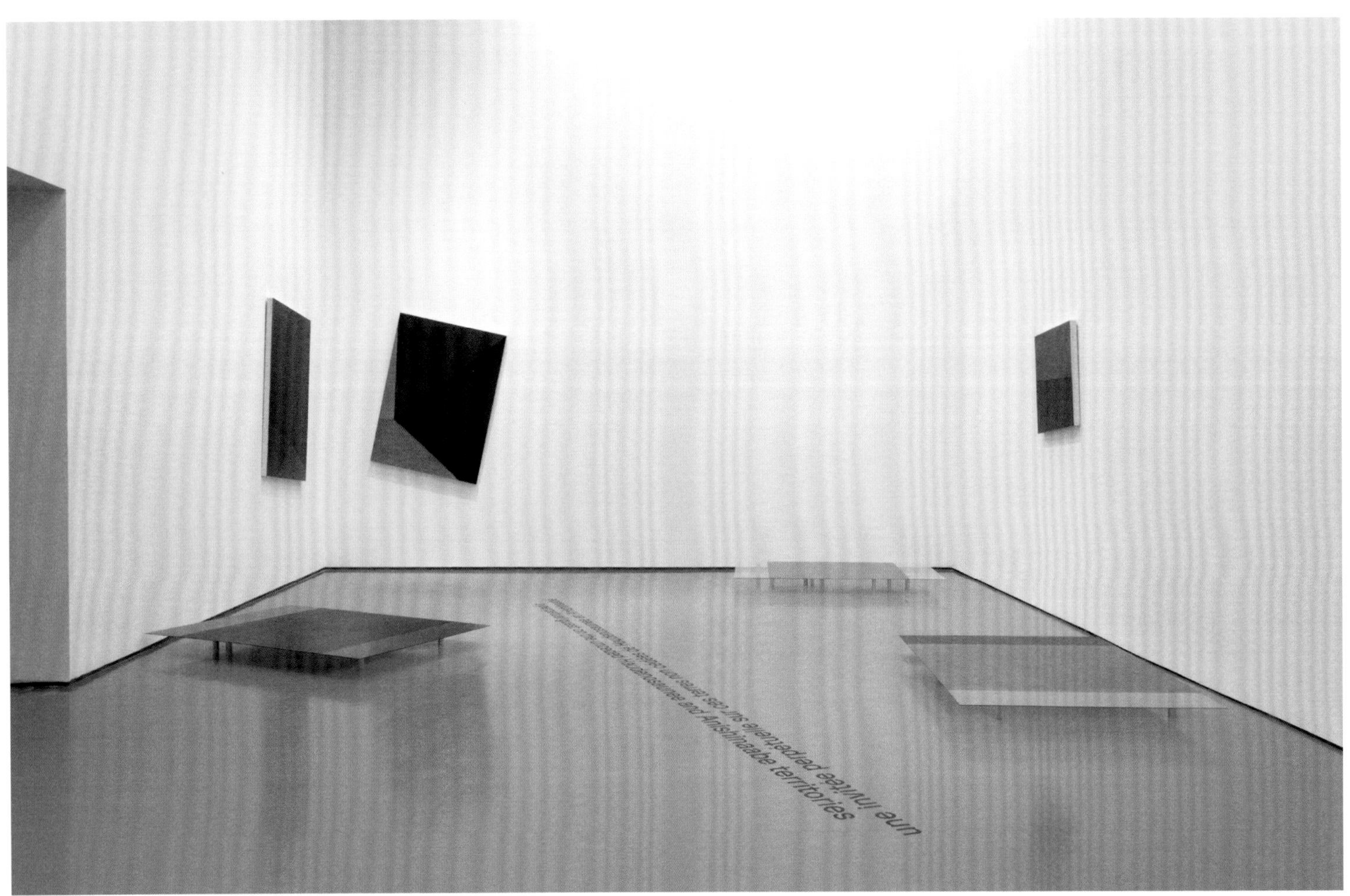

why does its lock fit my key?, 2018
oil on aluminium | huile sur aluminium
130 × 102 cm, 147 × 116 cm, 66 × 66 cm
and | et
Perpetual Guest, 2019
oil on glass and aluminium pilons |
huile sur vitre et pilons d'aluminium
10 × 152 × 102 cm

Installation view | vue d'installation,
RELATIONS: Diaspora and Painting |
RELATIONS: la diaspora et la peinture
July 8 – November 29, 2020 |
8 juillet – 29 novembre 2020
PHI Foundation for Contemporary Art |
Fondation PHI pour l'art contemporain,
Montréal

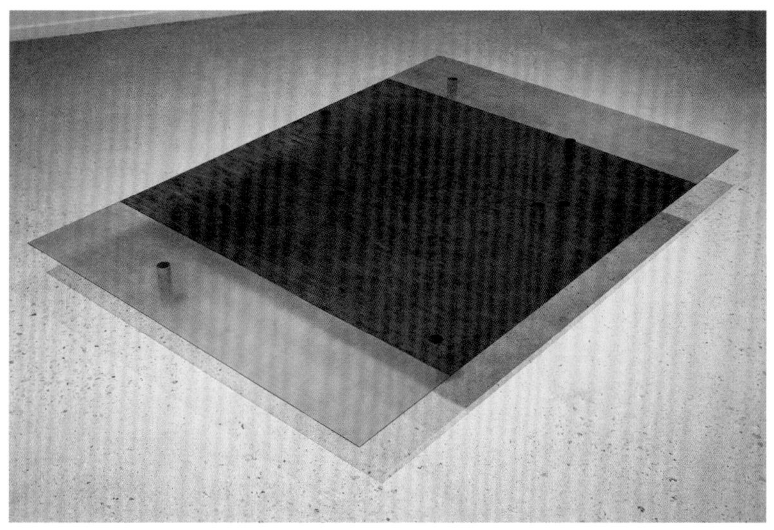

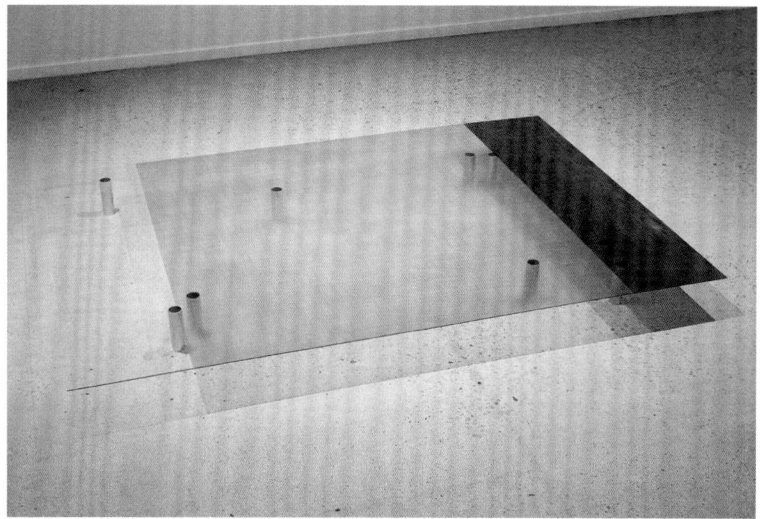

Perpetual Guest, 2019
oil on glass and aluminium pilons |
huile sur vitre et pilons d'aluminium
10 × 152 × 102 cm

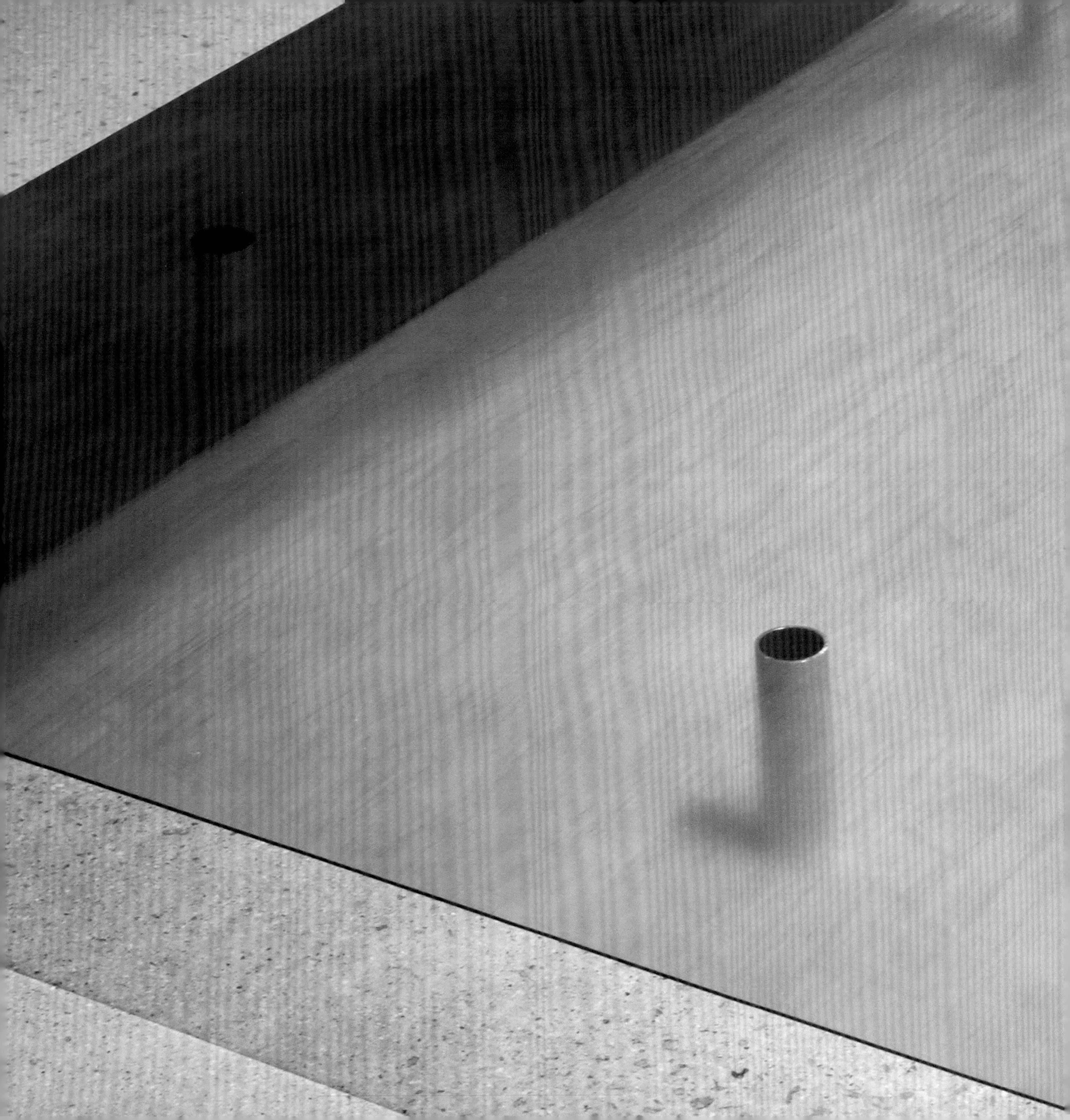

Perpetual Guest (detail | détail), 2019
oil on glass and aluminium pilons |
huile sur vitre et pilons d'aluminium
10 × 152 × 102 cm

L'instinct inhérent au champ de l'abstraction dans le monde de l'art se développe sur une promesse d'ouverture, particulièrement de résistance à ce qu'un artiste bien connu appelle le «fardeau du monde réel». Ce monde réel, cependant, aiguise également cet instinct qui est souvent réduit à la spécificité du médium de l'«abstrait». Certainement, la promesse d'ouverture, la résistance de l'instinct et les habitudes de reconnaissance institutionnelle ne devraient pas contraindre l'abstraction à n'importe quel point fixe qui s'avère pratique, que ce soit pour abréger la désignation ou pour saisir l'interprétation. Il devrait surgir, à travers ces éléments de tension génératrice, un moment de répit permettant à l'abstrait d'émerger à la limite.

Jinny Yu s'est confrontée à cette condition d'interrogation : chercher la lumière qui éclaire la manière dont la forme peut être stoppée dans sa dérive vers un terme, ou une prophétie préconçue. Plutôt, cette même lumière peut être envisagée comme taillant l'angle de la limite à travers laquelle la naissance de l'instinct trouve la chance de devenir particulière, parce qu'elle est précisément abstraite; son matériau n'est pas un poids inerte, mais le monde réel lui-même d'un autre domaine.

Une partie de cette limite consiste à ressentir la forme indéfinie que Yu tire de la multitude de ses inspirations ainsi que des urgences de la société environnante. Ainsi, en tant qu'étudiant de son art, j'essaie également une autre façon d'écrire avec et à travers elle, aux côtés d'une autre artiste qu'elle a rencontrée lors de ses études d'art à Montréal. Il s'agit de Lani Maestro (née 1957), une Philippine qui a émigré au Canada dans les années 1980. Tout comme je partage une partie de la subjectivité culturelle de Maestro, elle fait partie de la trajectoire de Yu en tant qu'artiste. À travers le texte de Maestro et ma réponse à celui-ci, un essai sur l'abstraction pourrait se configurer en relation avec les propositions de l'œuvre de Yu à travers les années.

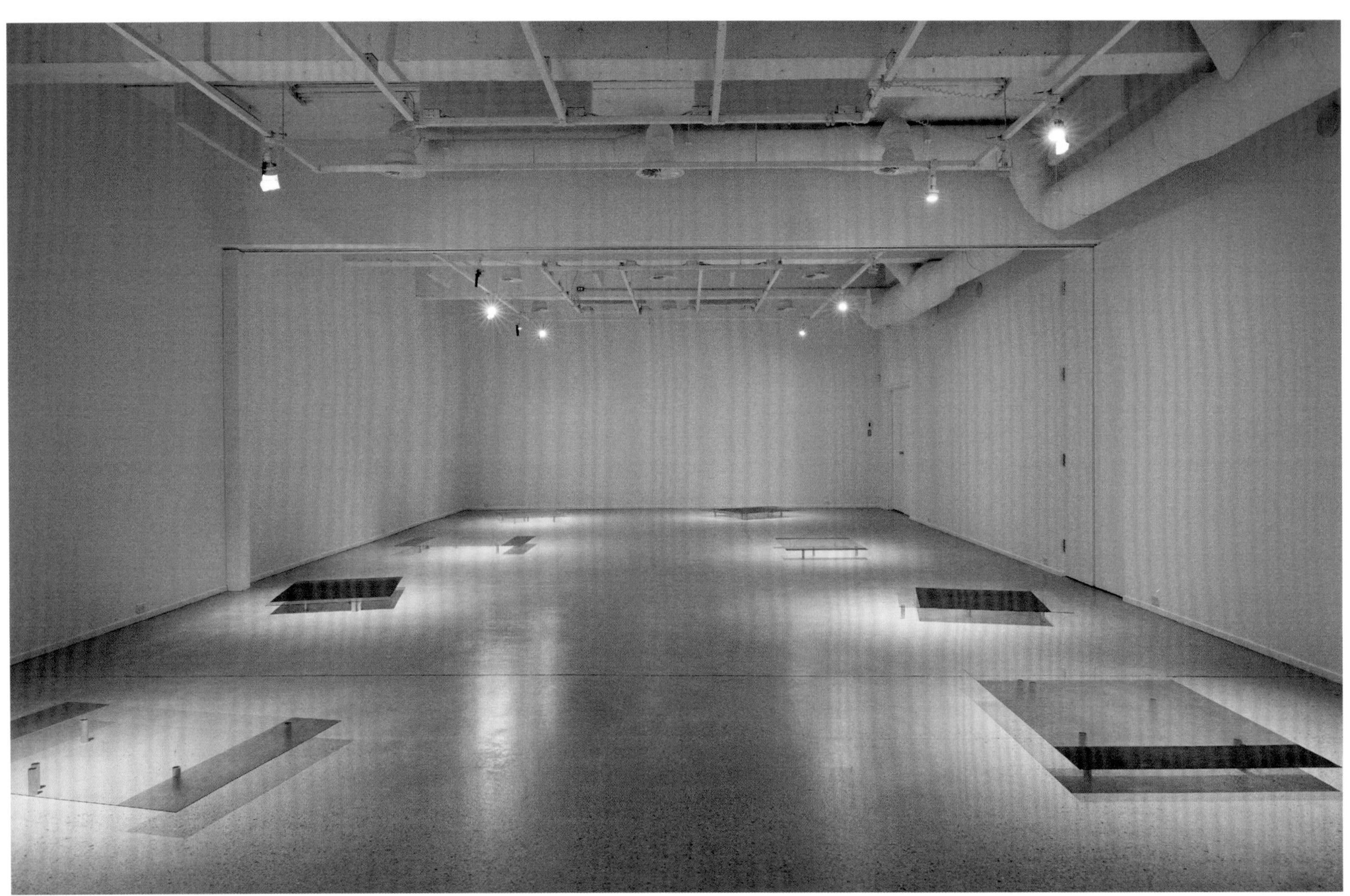

Installation view | vue d'installation
Perpetual Guest
November 6 – December 7, 2019 |
6 novembre – 7 décembre 2019
Galerie UQO, Gatineau

D'après Yu :

> J'ai rencontré Lani à la fin des années 1990, pendant mes études de premier cycle à l'Université Concordia de Montréal. Lani et son conjoint de l'époque nous avaient invités, moi et mon ami qui terminait sa maîtrise en production cinématographique à la même université, dans leur maison du Plateau. Si je me souviens bien, Lani enseignait l'un des cours de mon ami. J'ai été surpris qu'une professeure invite un étudiant et son amie chez elle et je me suis sentie honorée d'y être accueillie. Sa maison chaleureuse se trouvait dans l'un de ces duplex typiques du Plateau. Nous sommes entrés dans son salon depuis les rues gelées de Montréal et nous nous sommes assis sur son canapé pour discuter, grignoter et boire. Je ne me souviens pas vraiment de ce qui s'est dit, mais je me souviens d'elle comme d'une personne très généreuse et d'une hôtesse gracieuse. Mon ami, dont l'anglais était limité, car il venait de la Corée du Sud en passant par la France, parlait souvent de la générosité de sa professeure et mentore. Nous avons tous deux pensé qu'elle serait un bon modèle pour nous, d'autant plus qu'elle était la seule professeure non blanche avec laquelle nous avions interagi jusqu'alors. Mes contacts avec elle se sont limités à quelques visites, mais pendant les courts moments que j'ai passés chez elle, je me suis senti la bienvenue, confortable et à l'aise.[1]

Ce témoignage de contact et de rencontre entre deux artistes issus de l'immigration est essentiel pour créer l'atmosphère de l'abstraction comme une atmosphère d'ouverture, une hospitalité qui dissipe un hiver rigoureux ou la densité d'une langue étrangère. Lorsque j'ai parlé de Yu à Maestro, elle a eu du mal à s'en souvenir, mais elle a confirmé le sentiment partagé et l'expérience mutuelle d'un travail sur une subjectivité à la fois trouble et rétablie :

> ce qu'elle a raconté est vrai, car j'ai essayé d'accueillir les étudiants étrangers, en particulier ceux qui ne parlaient pas très bien l'anglais. en outre, il y avait un clivage entre les francophones et les anglophones et j'ai fait de mon mieux pour combler ce « fossé ». à l'époque, les discussions sur les politiques d'identité, c'est-à-dire la race et le genre, étaient intéressantes. elles étaient également troublantes et passionnantes pour les étudiants et les enseignants. j'ai ressenti le pouvoir d'action des étudiants qui ont gagné en confiance dans leur exploration du « soi ». j'ai beaucoup appris de cet échange et j'ai travaillé dur pour parvenir à une position moins clivante, moins idéologique . . . et j'ai toujours fait des œuvres d'art, la priorité dans l'exploration de leurs subjectivités.[2]

1 Correspondance par courriel avec l'auteur, 14 juillet 2023.

2 Correspondance par courriel avec l'auteur, 30 juillet 2023. La citation conserve la composition en bas de casse originale de Maestro.

Ces réminiscences de Yu et de Maestro sont des annotations de la pratique et alimentent une réflexion possible sur l'abstraction dans l'histoire et en tant que moyen de fabriquer des objets et d'interagir avec des personnes. En d'autres termes, la subjectivité qui est en jeu dans le travail de l'artiste est la matérialité de la forme elle-même, l'agentivité de sa sensualité. Le défi est de savoir comment transmettre ces énergies dans un certain exercice textuel. L'exploration de la forme abstraite par Yu est primordiale à cet égard. Cette forme se compose principalement d'ardoises délicatement inscrites, ou mieux, barbouillées ou tachées de pigment ou de graphite, mais parfois aussi envahies par des marques frénétiques comme s'il s'agissait d'étourneaux voyageurs. Il y a dans cette démarche la volonté de dépasser les champs binaires comme les vides et les enfermements, ou les espaces positifs et négatifs, les impressions de dimension ou les signes de l'abîme. L'artiste recherche plutôt une alternance ou une contiguïté de tons et d'angles, de bords et de gestes, de plis et de convergences, de superpositions pour former des réseaux, des vibrations ou des résonances, voire des ornements. Dans un cas, de la peinture sur verre transparent est suspendue, mais se trouve à proximité du sol en béton, séparée par de l'aluminium. La géométrie de Yu, bien que rigoureuse, s'aventure librement dans des variations chromatiques décisives, des permutations d'habitats potentiels, des gradations de la pression de sa main ou dans la façon dont la lumière s'échappe d'une fente faite de lignes faibles, mais indestructibles, à la fois sinueuses et tranquillement agitées. Ici et là, un semblant de portail palpite, avançant ou reculant dans un cosmos cendré, ou un texte polémique bouscule l'intelligence confortable. Si l'on était tenté de nommer les apparitions, elles pourraient être des pièces, des meubles ou un manifeste, familiers mais jamais banals. Éventuellement, cette grammaire de l'abstraction se dilue dans l'installation, élargissant la latitude et la sensation potentielle de la peinture ancienne.

La rencontre entre Yu et Maestro préfigurait le désir de la première pour la posture installative. Cela s'est déroulé dans un loft que Maestro avait construit pour des rassemblements dans un complexe abritant une communauté artistique. Ce loft est un espace curieux, généralement en porte-à-faux, suspendu comme un pont, mais qui conserve son volume en flottant. À bien des égards, il s'agit de ce que Derrida pourrait appeler un supplément, quelque chose qui n'est pas ajouté pour étendre la structure existante ou extraire un noyau, mais qui suit un autre chemin pour créer une autre proximité et rassembler les gens, en mettant en lumière ou en exposant le manque qui n'a pas tant besoin d'être comblé que

Tiepolo Project (detail | détail), 2011
oil on aluminum | huile sur aluminium
164 × 1341 × 483 cm
Confederation Centre Art Gallery Collection |
Collection du Musée d'art du Centre
de la Confédération, Charlottetown

Installation view | vue d'installation
Cadenza, March 23 – May 26, 2013 |
23 mars – 26 mai 2013
St. Mary's University Art Gallery, Halifax

d'être le début d'une autre relation qui aborde et, espérons-le, surmonte l'altérité ou l'identité, sans pour autant les rabâcher.

À bien des égards, un tel travail d'abstraction est une éthique de l'appartenance, un effort constant pour marquer à la fois une limite et un commencement. Comme le souligne Yu : « Le sentiment d'appartenance conduit souvent, selon moi, à un plus grand sens des responsabilités. Ainsi, par exemple, une colone bien implantée et soucieuse de protéger le territoire, ressentira- t-elle, avec les peuples autochtones, une responsabilité envers la terre plutôt que de chercher uniquement à en extraire les ressources? Ou un simple sentiment de respect de la part d'une invitée est-il meilleur et suffisant? Une invitée perpétuelle devrait-elle développer un sentiment d'appartenance?[3] »

La promesse de cette appartenance pourrait bien être l'accomplissement d'une intuition politique, bien que le parcours ait pu commencer à partir d'un site étrange. Il s'agit d'un lieu spirituel, spécifiquement catholique. L'expérience de résidence de Yu à Venise entre 2005 et 2016, son immersion dans une architecture de peintures et sa dévotion intense et quotidienne aux images, l'ont marquée au point de l'amener à « rejeter l'idée que la peinture est autonome, contenue seulement dans ses quatre coins. Je me suis rendu compte que la peinture devait interagir avec l'espace dans lequel elle se trouvait et qu'elle était toujours affectée par celui-ci.[4] » Cette inquiétude se concrétise lorsqu'elle examine de près le vieillissement de l'œuvre de Tiepolo (né 1696) dans laquelle c'est à travers l'indice du temps, à la manière de l'usure matérielle, qu'un espace ouvre l'entreprise moderniste à une précarité essentielle, qui se révèle comme ayant une généalogie chrétienne ainsi qu'une postérité postcoloniale de réappropriation.

Dans un compte-rendu de son engagement avec le *Serpent d'airain* (1731-1732) de Tiepolo, une peinture de jugement et de punition, elle explique comment l'œuvre devient contemporaine lorsqu'elle est libérée du fantasme de l'autonomie :

> C'étaient plutôt les fissures et les stries qui étaient les plus marquantes pour moi dans ce tableau. Lorsque je l'ai vu ici à la Gallerie dell'Accademia en 2008, j'ai réfléchi à la relation entre l'espace illusionniste et l'espace réel, ainsi qu'à la matérialité picturale. La strie est fondamentalement dépourvue de peinture, elle est donc physiquement plus éloignée du spectateur (aussi microscopique soit-elle) que la surface du tableau, qui décrit un espace illusionniste. Ce qui

3 *entretiens # 3: conversation between amy fung, david garneau and jinny yu on perpetual guest* (Gatineau : Galerie de l'UQO, 2019), p. 9.

4 *Jinny Yu : To Activate Space* (Montréal : Éditions Art Mûr, 2014), p. 35.

> m'intéressait, c'est que la strie qui est physiquement plus éloignée de nous est visuellement plus proche de nous, et que la surface peinte qui est physiquement proche de nous représente en fait un espace au-delà de cette surface. Au fond, pour moi, ce tableau de Tiepolo était la peinture contemporaine.[5]

Le fait que Yu discerne un manque de fluidité interne, ou intrinsèque, et qu'elle élargisse ainsi le champ de l'abstraction, ne peut être attribué qu'à son attention à la sémiose et au socius qui se fusionnent en même temps que l'artiste pense abstraitement, pratique l'abstraction, et se montre sensible à l'ambiance de l'œuvre, par exemple le son et le vent, qui sont des contingences essentielles qui rendent l'art chargé et en phase, présent de manière convaincante parmi les forces qui l'entourent.

Au-delà du formalisme de l'abstraction, il y a donc sa phénoménologie, évoquée avec acuité par le sensorium offert par la sensibilité de l'artiste à l'aluminium en tant que support qui absorbe l'environnement et résiste néanmoins à la gravité et à la bureaucratie de la peinture, laquelle n'est pas totalement assimilée par une surface métallique qui peut entièrement surdéterminer le champ visuel avec une figuration reconnaissable, ou une image, ou certaines identités à la fois de l'art et de son praticien. Cela nous rappelle comment l'abstractionniste Suzan Frecon (née 1941) a également été distraite, absorbée, presque envoûtée par le tableau lumineux de la *Vierge à l'Enfant* (vers 1290-1300) du peintre siennois médiéval Duccio : « Il me fait sortir de moi-même... Je m'y perds », disait-elle en observant le tableau comme « toujours en état de suspension.[6] »

Selon le critique et théoricien Richard Shiff, cette suspension est l'intervalle entre l'écologie et la conscience, la mémoire de la formation : « Contrebalançant la base mathématique invisible, sa surface visible est organique et irrégulière, comme si elle travaillait contre elle-même... À cette géométrie excentrique, elle ajoute les vibrations actives du rendu manuel. Sa peinture, en particulier le long des contours ellipsoïdaux, développe une apparence irrégulière... Sa composition... pourrait bien être vécue comme une anticomposition[7] ». Frecon considère que ce caractère insaisissable découle d'une impossibilité : « Il est impossible de dire que nous ne sommes pas issus de la nature[8] ».

5 Ibid, p.38.
6 Suzan Frecon, « Suspension », dans *Richard Shiff, Writing after Art: Essays on Modern and Contemporary Artists* (New York: David Zwirner Books, 2023), p. 199.
7 Ibid., p. 203.
8 Ibid.

Tiepolo Project (detail | détail), 2011
oil on aluminum | huile sur aluminium
164 × 1280 × 61 cm
Confederation Centre Art Gallery Collection | Collection du Musée d'art du Centre de la Confédération, Charlottetown

Installation view | vue d'installation
Cadenza, September 2 – November 5, 2011 | 2 septembre – 5 novembre 2011
McMaster Museum of Art, Hamilton

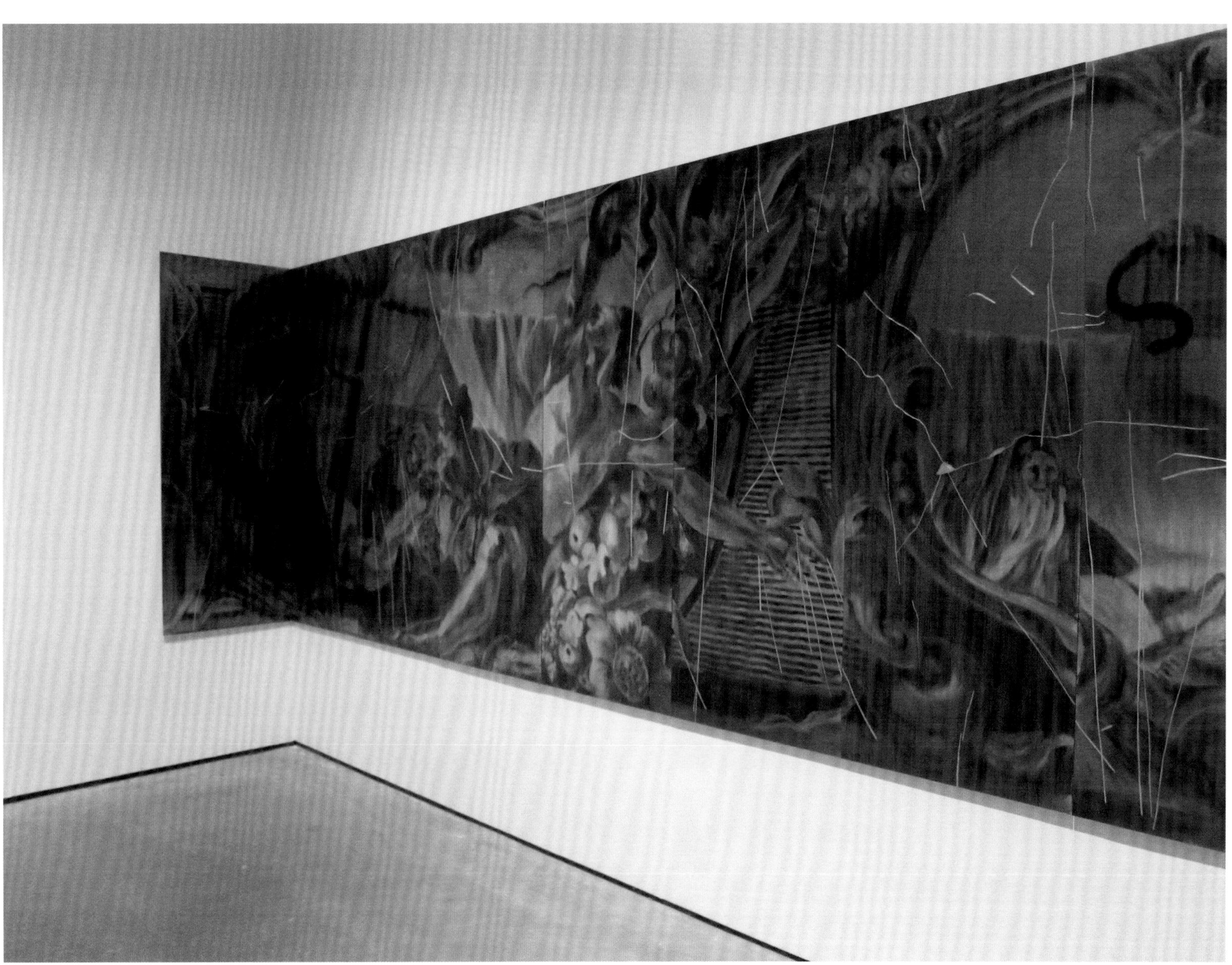

Les premières incursions de Maestro en peinture étaient des abstractions, qu'elle compare à un tissage par leur complexité poignante et délibérée, ainsi que par la persistance de matrices vulnérables qui, comme les propres mailles granuleuses de Yu, laissent la lumière filtrer légèrement, ou du moins refléter une lueur, ou faire allusion à de l'eau, ou à une sorte de précipitation. À partir de ces peintures, elle est devenue plus attentive et sensible à la réminiscence, ou à la membrane, des lignes. Considérons la façon dont elle décrit son travail *Sing Mother (Twilight eats you)* :

> *sing mother (twilight eats you)* est une série de dessins à l'encre qui a vu le jour après une visite en corée il y a quelques années. en 2004, je suis allée voir la dmz, la zone démilitarisée qui délimite la frontière entre le sud et le nord. je voulais ressentir quelque chose de l'histoire de mon père, un officier militaire qui a combattu dans la guerre de corée en 1952. d'où je me trouvais, une atmosphère de désolation enveloppait ce territoire miné restreint, stérile et menaçant, hérissé de kilomètres de fils barbelés à double clôture et surveillé par des gardes armés. un phénomène intéressant s'est manifesté alors que cette longue bande de terre est devenue un lieu de réflexion sur les politiques qui maintiennent ce pays divisé. elle est devenue un sanctuaire pour des espèces rares douées de sentience.
>
> cet espace liminal est devenu un lieu de refuge, car je n'arrivais pas à retrouver un quelconque lien avec les représentations muséologiques de la guerre dans le musée. j'ai commencé à dessiner en essayant de repeindre la série de peintures de fleurs de ma mère et le travail a évolué vers cette série de «dessins d'abandon». comme certaines œuvres antérieures, *sing mother* émane d'un narratif quelconque, mais l'histoire échappe au récit puisqu'elle permet à d'autres subjectivités de se dévoiler…
>
> je considère cette «trahison» dans le langage comme quelque chose de positif dans la récupération de soi, car elle rend l'expérience de l'altérité, de l'inconnu, beaucoup plus apparente, plus ressentie. elle pose également la question de l'inadéquation de la représentation de la réalité telle que nous la vivons. je trouve que l'espace liminal du savoir et du non-savoir est une abstraction à laquelle nous parvenons souvent si nous voulons rester ouverts à la complexité du monde en tant qu'événement. le régime de représentation qui marque notre appréhension de l'histoire est ce vers quoi mon travail semble souvent se diriger et ce qu'il aborde inconsciemment — cette ligne/espace palpitante qui marque l'expérience et le langage qui évolue pour former ce que nous appelons la «mémoire».

> les mots ont toujours été présents dans mon travail sous forme de dessins, de lignes, d'idées ou de sources d'inspiration invisibles. souvent, c'est dans les failles de la communication, dans les tentatives de créer un lien avec l'autre, qu'il soit humain ou non humain, que je trouve l'existence sensuelle de la poésie.[9]

Les œuvres récentes de Yu, réalisées avec de la peinture à l'huile sur panneaux d'aluminium, de la gouache et de l'aquarelle sur papier, conservent la délicatesse avec laquelle l'artiste a utilisé le vocabulaire de l'abstraction. L'algorithme des formes en interaction et des matrices rectilignes changeantes évoque ses recherches sur les liens entre l'hôte et l'invité dans une situation de migration, de labeur réciproque, bien que difficile, qui sous-tend des générosités difficiles dans un contexte de racisme systémique, ainsi que d'amitiés et de gentillesse profondes. La névrose moderniste concernant la planéité de la surface trouve un contrepoint, comme dans une polyphonie, dans des suggestions de rondeur et un investissement dans le rythme par l'artiste. Les couches de glacis minces, apparemment disposées avec une discipline remarquable, évoquent une certaine brillance ou lustre, même lorsque la polychromie lyrique prédomine et tend à hypnotiser. Une telle transparence, qui est aussi une iridescence, peut rappeler une enfance avec des jouets ou même une table garnie de gelée pour dessert!

Cette insistance et cette patience à inscrire en surface soutiennent fondamentalement les enjeux complexes d'être actuel et pertinent dans un monde qui exclut, discrimine et aliène, ainsi que dans un art qui, comme les «gestes effrontés» dans l'abstraction naissante de Maestro, est capable de signifier l'impossibilité de la présence ou le désaveu d'un contenu susceptible d'être instrumentalisé. Cela dit, la femme artiste qui s'engage dans l'abstraction joue aussi le jeu de la visibilité, de la tactique délicate de la représentation dans la mesure où elle convie «le vent, le ciel et la pluie[10]». Si l'abstraction est finalement non objective, c'est parce que la femme artiste est le médium du subjectif.

Yu et Maestro recherchent toutes deux la joie de cette existence sensuelle, même si elles gravitent autour des problèmes de «l'autre», de la «structure», de la «nature». À la fois, la joie et les difficultés incitent et inspirent à concevoir l'abstraction légitime dans laquelle elles – les femmes, les migrantes et les artistes – peuvent véritablement vivre. ◆

9 Lani Maestro, lettre à Susan Gibson Garvey, 2006, gracieuseté de Lani Maestro.

10 Lani Maestro, échange courriel avec l'auteur, 10 octobre 2023.

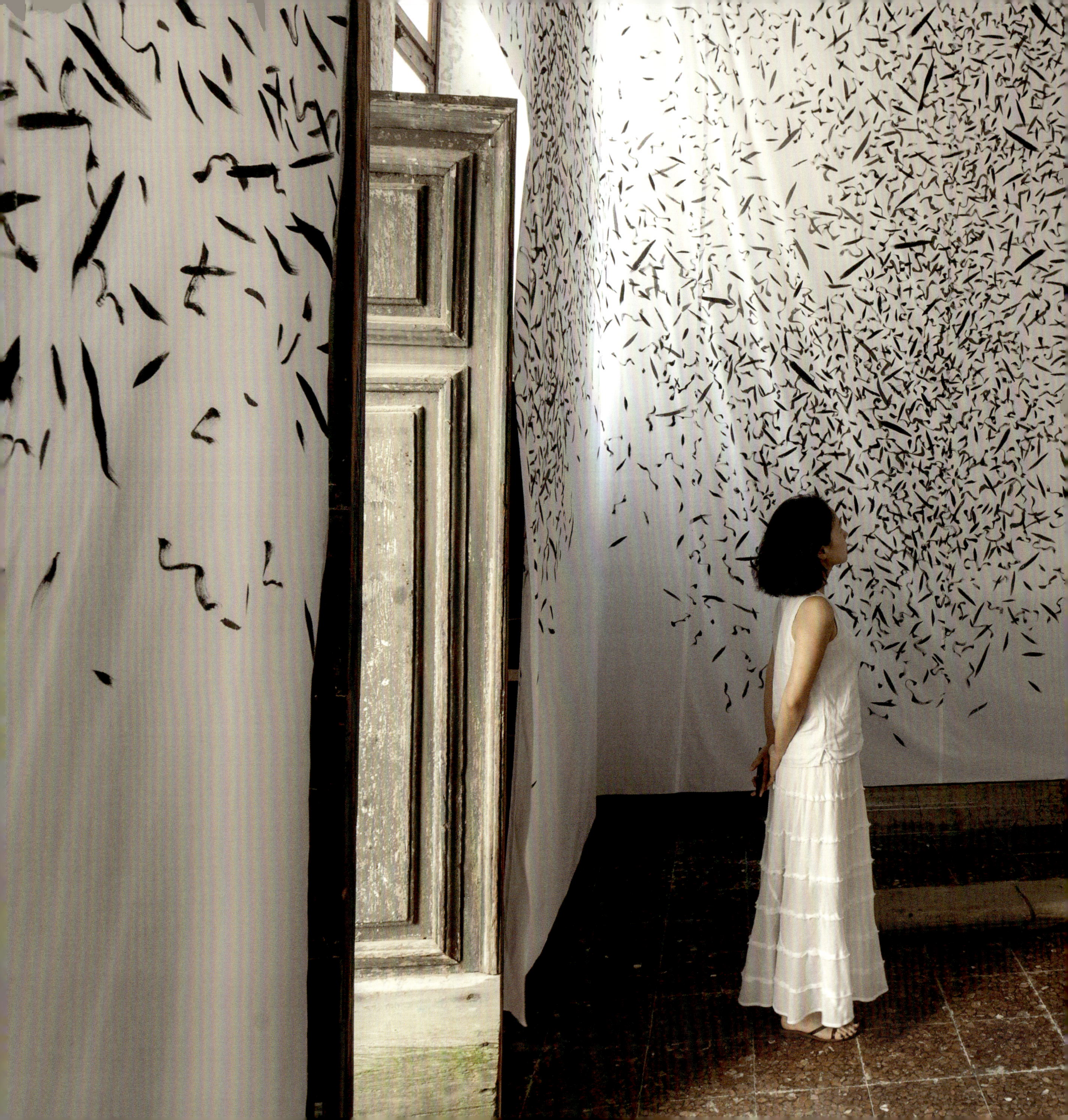

Jinny Yu: In a World of Binaries, the Pluriversal

Ming Tiampo

Jinny Yu : Dans un monde binaire, le pluriversel

Ming Tiampo

Don't They Ever Stop Migrating?, 2015
ink on fabric and sound | encre sur tissu et son
521 × 541 × 389 cm
Agnes Etherington Art Centre Collection |
Collection Agnes Etherington Art Centre, Kingston

Installation view | vue d'installation
Don't They Ever Stop Migrating?
September 5 – November 22, 2015 |
5 septembre – 22 novembre 2015
Nuova Icona, 56th Venice Biennale |
56e Biennale de Venise

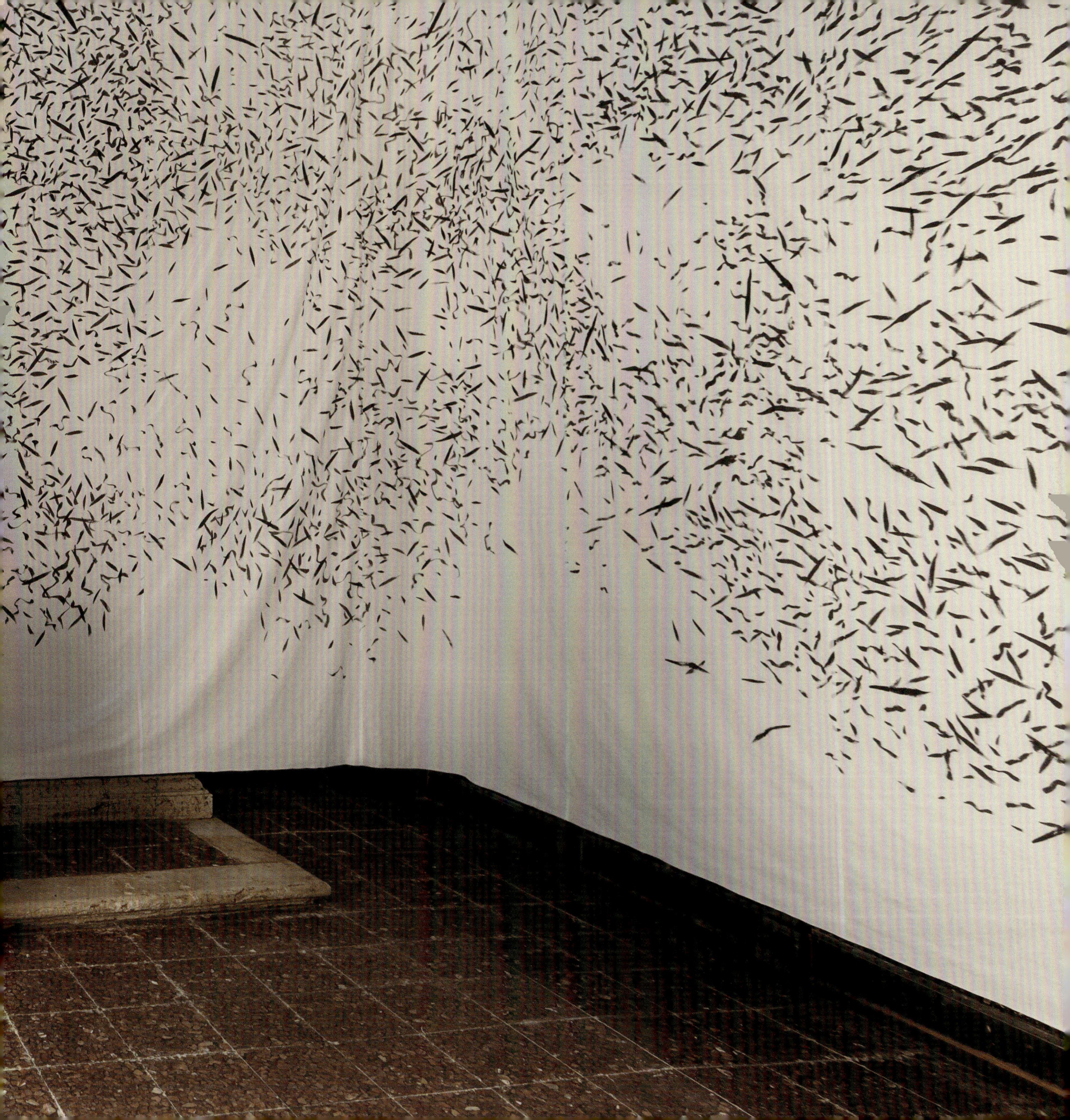

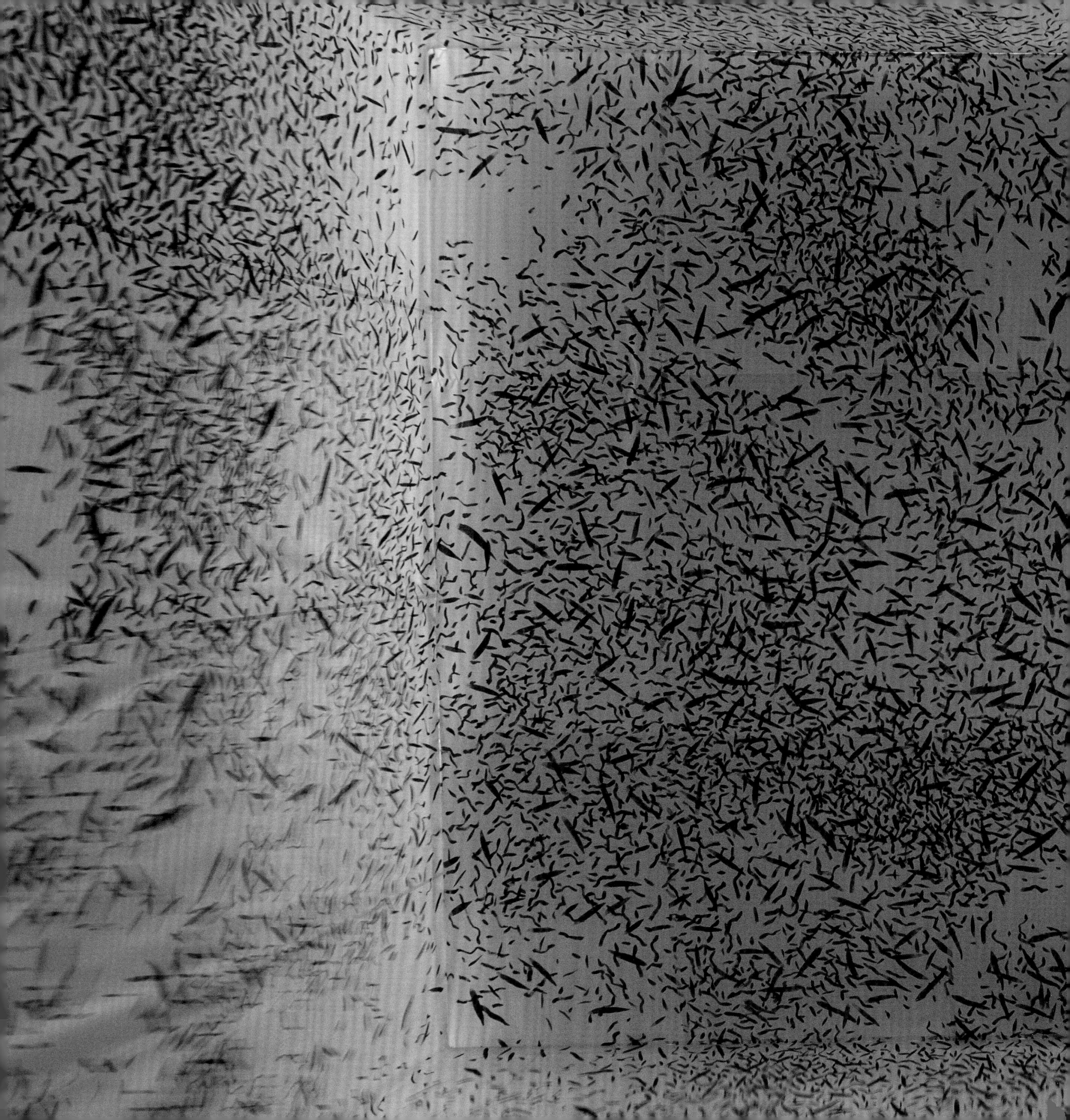

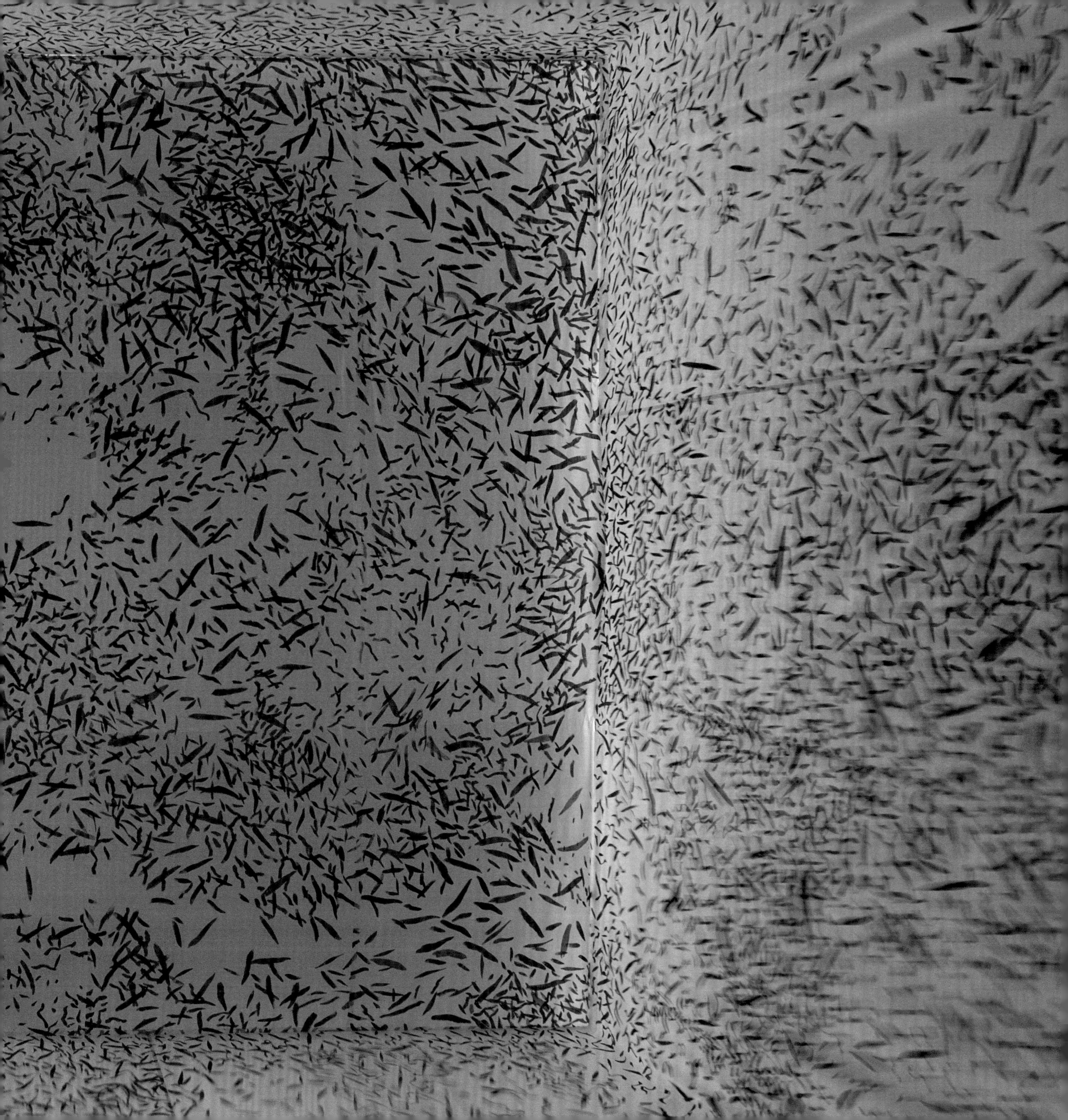

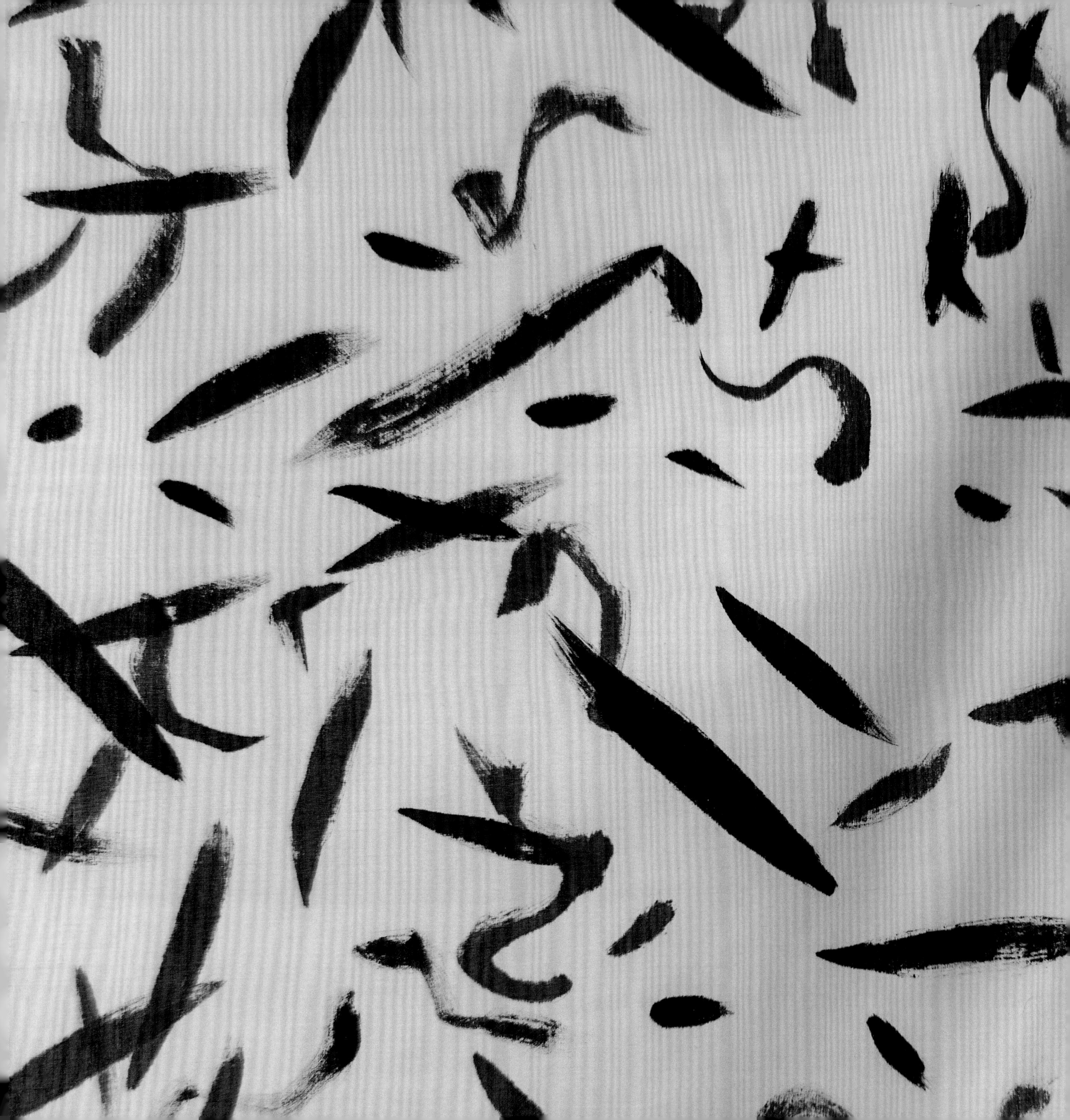

↑ *Don't They Ever Stop Migrating?*, 2015
ink on fabric and sound | encre sur tissu et son
521 × 541 × 389 cm
Agnes Etherington Art Centre Collection |
Collection Agnes Etherington Art Centre, Kingston

← *Don't They Ever Stop Migrating?*
(detail | détail), 2015
ink on fabric and sound | encre sur tissu et son
521 × 541 × 389 cm
Agnes Etherington Art Centre Collection |
Collection Agnes Etherington Art Centre, Kingston

Jinny Yu's paintings demand that we slow down and pay attention, to look in a way that we have forgotten how to look. To allow ourselves to see beyond the discursive *what* in an attention economy that asks only for superficial engagement, tiny slivers of time, and distracted glances. Yu's paintings do not shout, but they ask that we look, that we listen, and that we critically reflect beyond surfaces in order to deeply question and reimagine structures.

At first glance, the works are deceptively formalist, and seem to participate in a Modernist conversation about painting that, while laying claim to a co-created and transnational history of form that deftly weaves together Geometric Abstraction, Minimalism, Dansaekhwa, and Mono-ha, seems not to be explicitly political. Yu's paintings are not, however, pure form, but rather use an inquiry into form as a portal for conceptual and political reflection. Painting on cotton that moves on air currents like breath, glass that reveals the ground beneath like desire, and aluminum panels that appear and disappear like light, Yu is an artist who explores the thresholds of painting as a means of probing the borders that we construct in ourselves, in the ways that we organize the world, and in the conceptual frameworks we use to understand art, life, and politics.

> "The world is burning, and I am painting."
> —Jinny Yu

Can abstract art be political? Can political art be abstract? What is the relationship between aesthetics and politics? How do Yu's paintings, which delve deeply into questions that reverberate within the hermetic field of painting *qua* painting, also resonate beyond, making waves that ripple outwards to change the way that we think about ourselves in the world, on this land, and in relation to others? How does Yu activate the capacities of abstraction to formulate new ways of being and knowing?[1] How do these paintings provide viewers with an affective and formal language for imagining the world otherwise (in other ways, as well as through other forms of wisdom), in a pluriversal world beyond binaries and incommensurable positions?[2]

The political turn in Yu's work began with 2015's *Don't They Ever Stop Migrating?* an immersive painting installation created for an exhibition presented alongside *All the World's Futures*, the 56th Venice Biennale curated by Okwui Enwezor. In the context of this biennial, which was thinking about futures for all and not just for the few, Yu's work was an act of restorative justice that brought attention to the crisis of desperate migration in the Mediterranean, while also asking tough questions about the psychology behind fear and Othering.

The work consists of a series of soft cotton panels installed to create a room, painted with inked brushstrokes that cluster and disperse like murmurations. Accompanying the scatter of form is also a scatter of voices and hushed, anxious susurrations — a sound collage Yu created from Alfred Hitchcock's *The Birds* (1963) that creates an environment of panic: "Where did you come from? What are you? What's happening? I think you are the cause of this! You're frightening the children . . ." whispers a chorus of female voices. The oppressive fear evoked by the voices is not continuous, however, and the silences in between allow the viewer to see the soaring beauty of Yu's painting, its shape shifting with the air currents and opening worlds rather than closing them.

The tension between the world opening of the work's visual language and the xenophobia of its aural tonalities invites the viewer to reconsider the question of migration from multiple perspectives and positionalities. Rather than taking sides and creating silos, the work generously creates dialogue about what it means to fear the unknown, as well as offering the possibility of opening oneself up to other worlds, other positionalities, and other ways of knowing — a fact underscored by the work's medium, ink on cotton. Referencing East Asian materials and methods, the work questions the default position and centring of Western media such as oil or acrylic on canvas, making worlds through other materialities.

→ *Don't They Ever Stop Migrating?*, 2015
ink on fabric and sound | encre sur tissu et son
521 × 541 × 389 cm
Agnes Etherington Art Centre Collection |
Collection Agnes Etherington Art Centre, Kingston

Installation view | vue d'installation
Jinny Yu: Don't They Ever Stop Migrating?
May 7 – September 11, 2016 |
7 mai – 11 septembre 2016
The Rooms, St. John's

↘ *Don't They Ever Stop Migrating?*, 2015
ink on fabric and sound | encre sur tissu et son
521 × 541 × 389 cm
Agnes Etherington Art Centre Collection |
Collection Agnes Etherington Art Centre, Kingston

Installation view | vue d'installation
Don't They Ever Stop Migrating?
September 5 – November 22, 2015 |
5 septembre – 22 novembre 2015
Nuova Icona, 56th Venice Biennale |
56e Biennale de Venise

1 David Getsy, "Reduction as Expansion: the Queer Capacities of Abstract Art." Public lecture, ICI Berlin, February 1, 2021.

2 Wayne Modest, "World Art Studies and the Ethnographic Museum," lecture, Carleton University, October 10, 2023; Tiffany Lethabo King, Jenell Navarro, and Andrea Smith, eds., *Otherwise Worlds: Against Settler Colonialism and Anti-Blackness* (Durham: Duke University Press, 2020).

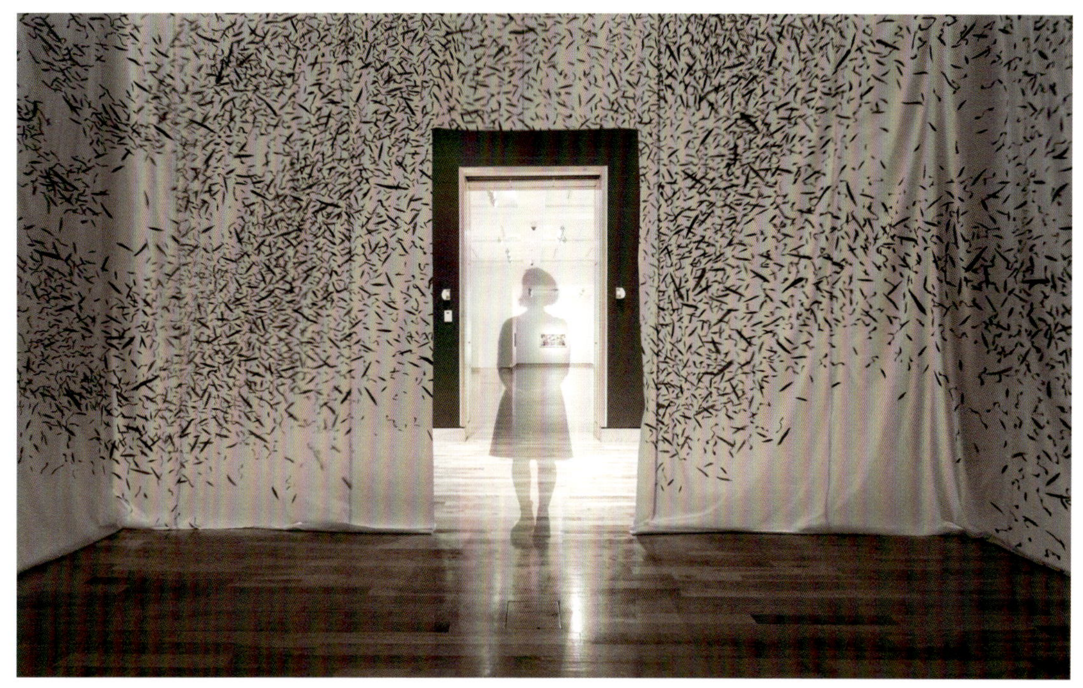

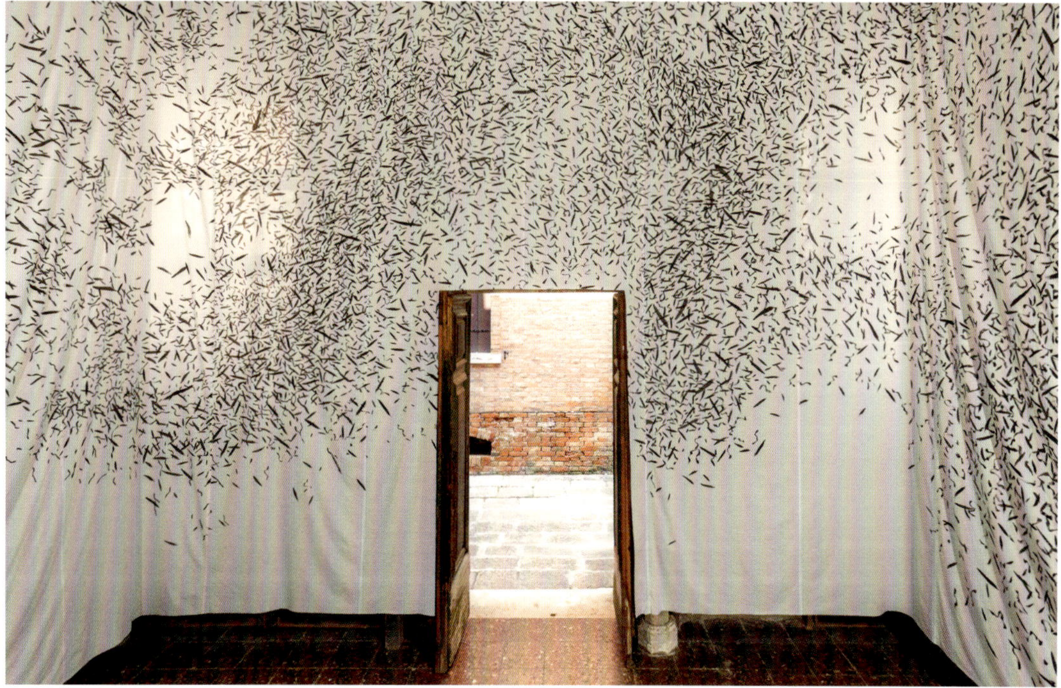

With *Perpetual Guest* (2019), Yu's own locus of inquiry shifted from a European context to a radical questioning of her relationship with the land on Turtle Island. In this work, the viewer's line of sight is pivoted from looking upwards in *Don't They Ever Stop Migrating?* to looking downwards, at the ground; from thinking about migrations to thinking about forms of emplacement and landing. The work consists of a series of paintings made with black oil on untempered glass panels propped precariously on aluminum pylons. Each panel is a ghostly presence, painted into three monochromatic zones of varying opacities, and floating horizontally about 10 cm from the ground. Employing what Métis artist David Garneau characterizes as a "hovering strategy — having more space but less footprint,"[3] these panels wrestle with the politics of claiming space in White institutions as an artist of colour, but resist the cognitive dissonance of settler-colonial emplacement. Indeed, when the work was first exhibited in 2019, at the Galerie UQO in Gatineau, Québec, it occupied a gallery that could not be entered without the viewer first walking over a text on the floor that read in French: "Jinny Yu: Perpetual Guest on these unceded lands of the Algonquin Anishinaabe Nation."

What does it mean though, to be a perpetual guest, to not only resist the presumed entitlements of belonging, but also to thus release oneself from the responsibilities of community? Yu's next series, *Hôte* (2020), embarked upon this question in a drawing cycle that she also made into an artist's book P.54,55. Layering oil-based graphite on paper in palimpsests of time, gesture, and material, Yu created forty-two drawings that resemble thresholds. These works draw upon Algerian-born French philosopher Jacques Derrida's reflections on *hôte*, which in French is a contranym that signifies both host and guest.[4] Cognizant of her own position as a welcomed guest of an unwelcome guest on Indigenous lands, Yu nonetheless challenges the problematic sense of limited responsibility that guests may perceive for themselves, seeking modes of belonging through responsibility rather than possession. She asks: "Can a guest host? Can a host guest?" The series begins with clear delineations between black and white, which stand in for host and guest, but as it progresses, the lines become increasingly more imbricated, until they transform into configurations of grey on grey. As anthropologist Tim

3 *entretiens # 3: conversation between amy fung, david garneau and jinny yu on perpetual guest*. Gatineau: Galerie UQO, 2019, 33.

4 Jacques Derrida and Anne Dufourmantelle, *Of Hospitality*. (Stanford: Stanford University Press, 2000).

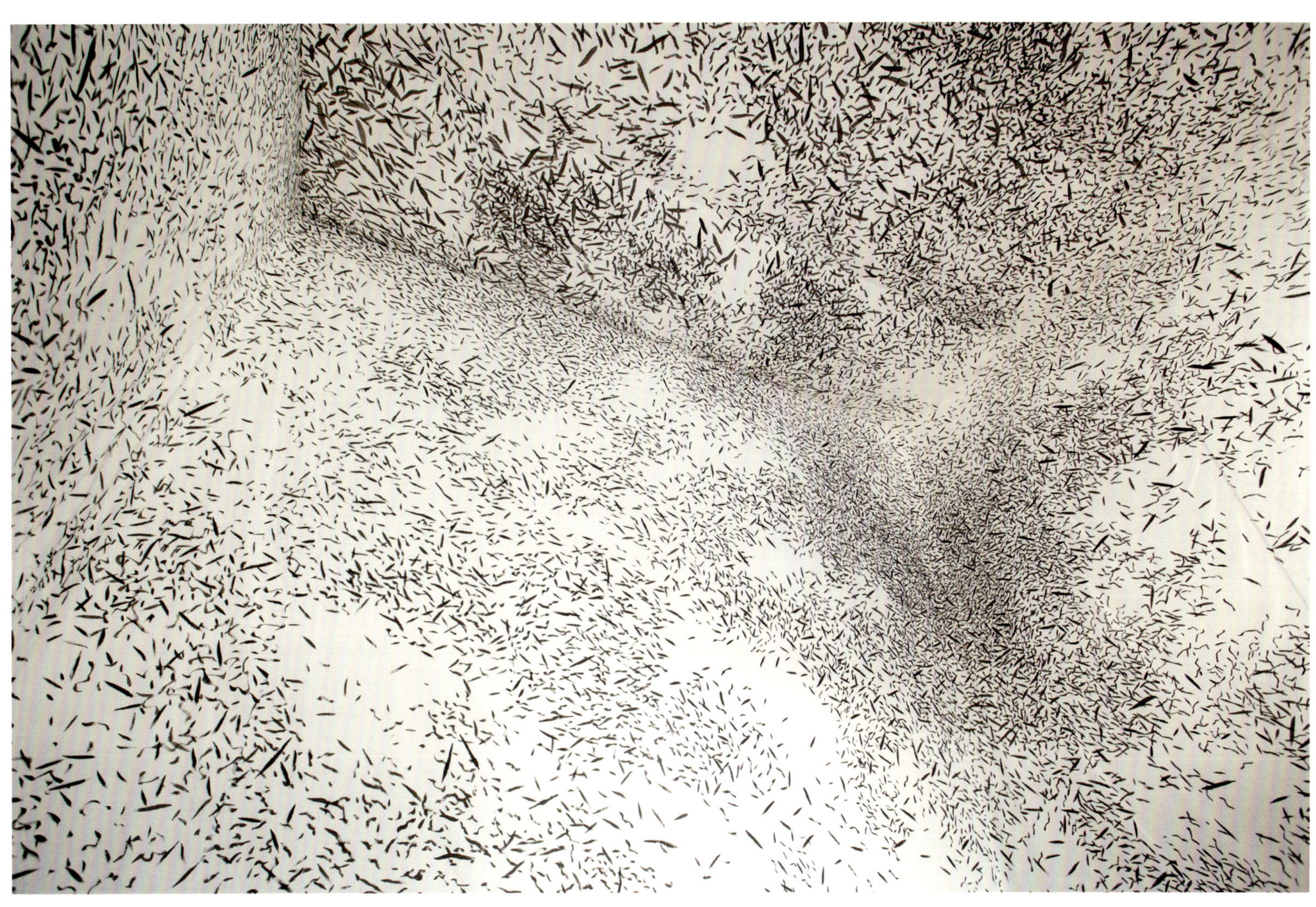

Don't They Ever Stop Migrating?, 2015
ink on fabric and sound | encre sur tissu et son
521 × 541 × 389 cm
Agnes Etherington Art Centre Collection |
Collection Agnes Etherington Art Centre, Kingston

Ingold wrote, "Souls, we might say, are answerable to one another, a condition that carries entailments of both responsiveness and responsibility."[5]

Yu develops *Hôte*'s contranym further, engaging with the question of relationality in the series *Inextricably Ours* (2021) through visual form. In this series, she paints geometric forms that are multistable figures, or *kippbilder*, the classic example being the duck/rabbit evoked by Ernst Gombrich in *Art and Illusion*, whose beak transforms into long ears with a shift in the viewer's perception. These forms, which optically shift between being figure and ground, allow for the coexistence of contradictory claims "without dissolving differences between conflicting accounts or establishing a higher synthesis."[6] It is here that Yu begins to imagine figure transforming into ground and back into figure, giving visual form to Derrida's reflections on *hôte* as a relationality of hospitality, care, and mutual respect. In this formulation, guest is as responsible to host as host is responsible to guest, with all of us as guests passing through this earthly world.

The work of attaining this level of relationality, of negotiating what Wanda Nanibush and Georgiana Uhlyarik describe as a decolonizing "treaty relationship" through broken pasts and difficult histories, is arduous and continuous.[7] In 2020, when *Perpetual Guest* was being exhibited, a visitor to the gallery stepped on the work, shattering it into shards. Yu had the pieces sent back to her studio where, under lockdown, she painstakingly assembled them into a new work *Perpetual Guest 2019/2022 Impossibility of Repair* (2023). An assemblage that does not use glue, the work is now marked by its deliberate temporariness and its relationship with the ground, the fissures now operating as sites of openness, friction, and constant reconfiguration, which fracture the distance previously performed by the wholeness of *Perpetual Guest*. Each of the fragments is its own entity, yet functions in intimate relation with blank spaces and other fragments to create landscapes and histories that are at once broken, multiple, and continuously reimagined.[8]

5 Tim Ingold, "One World Anthropology," HAU *Journal of Ethnographic Theory* 9, no. 1 (2018): 160.

6 Christoph Holzhey, ed., *Multistable Figures: On the Critical Potential of Ir/Reversible Aspect-Seeing* (Vienna: Turia + Kant, 2014), 7.

7 Wanda Nanibush and Georgiana Uhlyarik, eds., *Moving the Museum: Indigenous + Canadian Art at the* AGO (Fredericton: Goose Lane Editions; Toronto: Art Gallery of Ontario, 2023); Wanda Nanibush and Georgiana Uhlyarik, in *Worlding the Global: The Arts in the Age of Decolonization*, ed. Birgit Hopfener and Ming Tiampo (Berlin: ICI Berlin Press, forthcoming 2024).

8 Parts of this analysis are based upon the introduction to Birgit Hopfener and Ming Tiampo, *Worlding the Global: The Arts in the Age of Decolonization* (Berlin: ICI Berlin Press, forthcoming 2024).

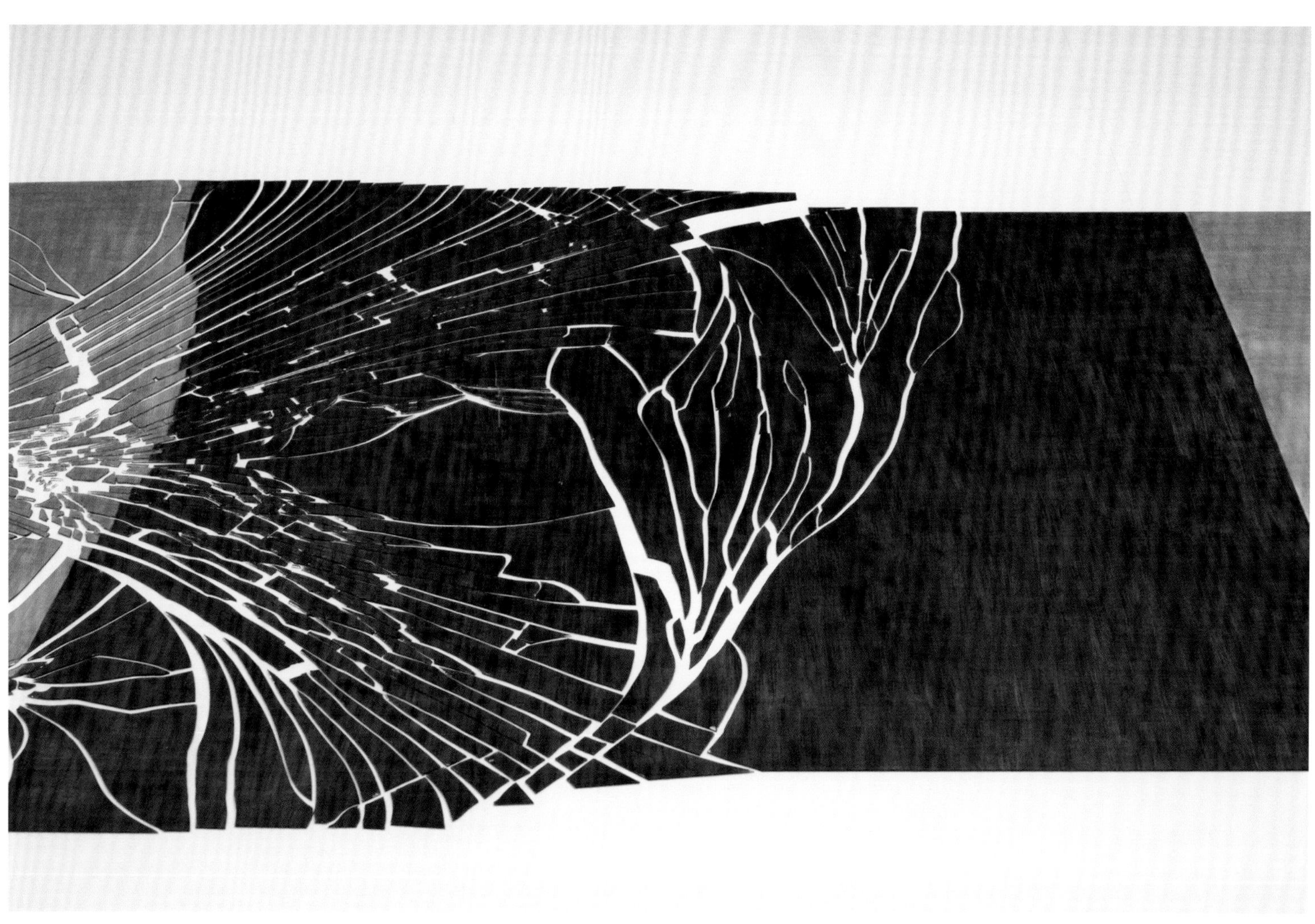

Perpetual Guest 2019/2022 Impossibility of Repair (detail | détail), 2023
oil on glass and platform | huile sur vitre et plateforme
4 × 366 × 305 cm

Mirroring the ways in which she allowed the world to enter in through the cracks of *Perpetual Guest*, Yu's practice opens itself up to an activist modality that is implicated in her painting. Perhaps the most important of her activities in collaborative practice, discursive curating, radical pedagogies and community organizing, is the Canadian BIPOC Artists Rolodex (CBIPOCAR), a digital humanities project that she initiated with Celina Jeffery and myself in dialogue with data curator Felicity Tayler.

CBIPOCAR is a re-envisaged database that makes visible BIPOC (Black, Indigenous, People of Colour) artists in Canada, and is designed to increase research, teaching, and exhibitions on BIPOC artists. As a Rolodex, the project is also about building relationships, and is conceived to connect BIPOC artists both digitally and through planned discursive activities. Yu initially conceived of CBIPOCAR in response to a claim that BIPOC artists are difficult to incorporate into a visual arts curriculum because they are so difficult to find. In the rising contexts of the Black Lives Matter, Idle No More, and Stop Asian Hate movements, however, the project became an important decolonial strategy to address the fact that BIPOC artists have little institutional saturation, are given fewer exhibitions, are less taught, and most importantly, are discursively less visible in histories and accounts of Canadian art.

In addition to the empirical projects of data collection and narration, CBIPOCAR is also necessarily engaged in critical data studies, seeking to decolonize assumptions made by data science about identity, medium, and even the nature and definitions of art. Who is included in an identity group? Who gets to decide? What nomenclature should we use? Who should have access to this information? What media should be indexed? How do we define art and what do we call it? Bringing together a nineteen-member advisory board of BIPOC artists, curators and academics, the project thus grapples with the similarities, differences, and entanglements of how members of these different groups operating in solidarity imagine category fields that are never neutral entities. Like the reconfiguration of *Perpetual Guest* from its fragments, these discussions question siloed binaries and reimagine possible relations, forms, landscapes, histories, and languages.

Operating otherwise, Yu's multifarious practice opens worlds through inquiry that proposes pluriversal ways of knowing and seeing, multistable figures that hold together multiple and sometimes conflicting realities: *At Once*.

At Once material and image
At Once concreteness and representation
At Once figure and ground
At Once the one and the many
At Once figurative and abstract
At Once objective and non-objective
At Once host and guest
At Once here and there
At Once painting and activism
At Once poetics and politics
At Once data and stories
At Once material and light
At Once clarity and opacities
At Once known and unknown
At Once seeing and reading
At Once sensing and knowing
At Once individual and group
At Once guest and host
At Once settler and colonized
At Once inheritances and futurities
At Once Self, Other, otherwise ■

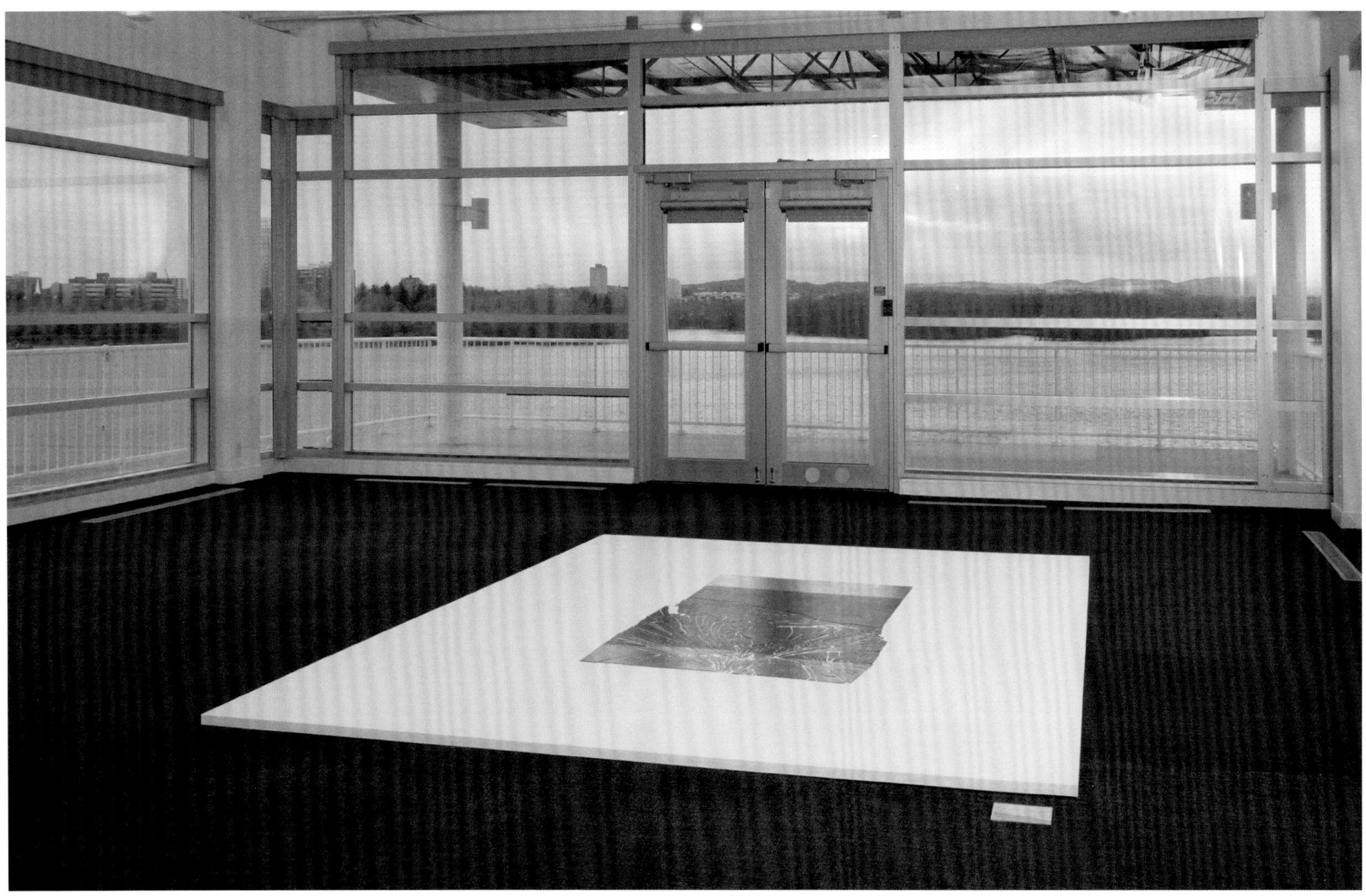

Perpetual Guest 2019/2022 Impossibility of Repair
(detail | détail), 2023
oil on glass and platform | huile sur vitre et plateforme
4 × 366 × 305 cm

Installation view | vue d'installation
Marina Roy, Jinny Yu & the Painted Object
October 27 – November 7, 2023 |
27 octobre – 7 novembre 2023
Royal Canadian Academy of Arts |
Académie royale des arts du Canada, Ottawa

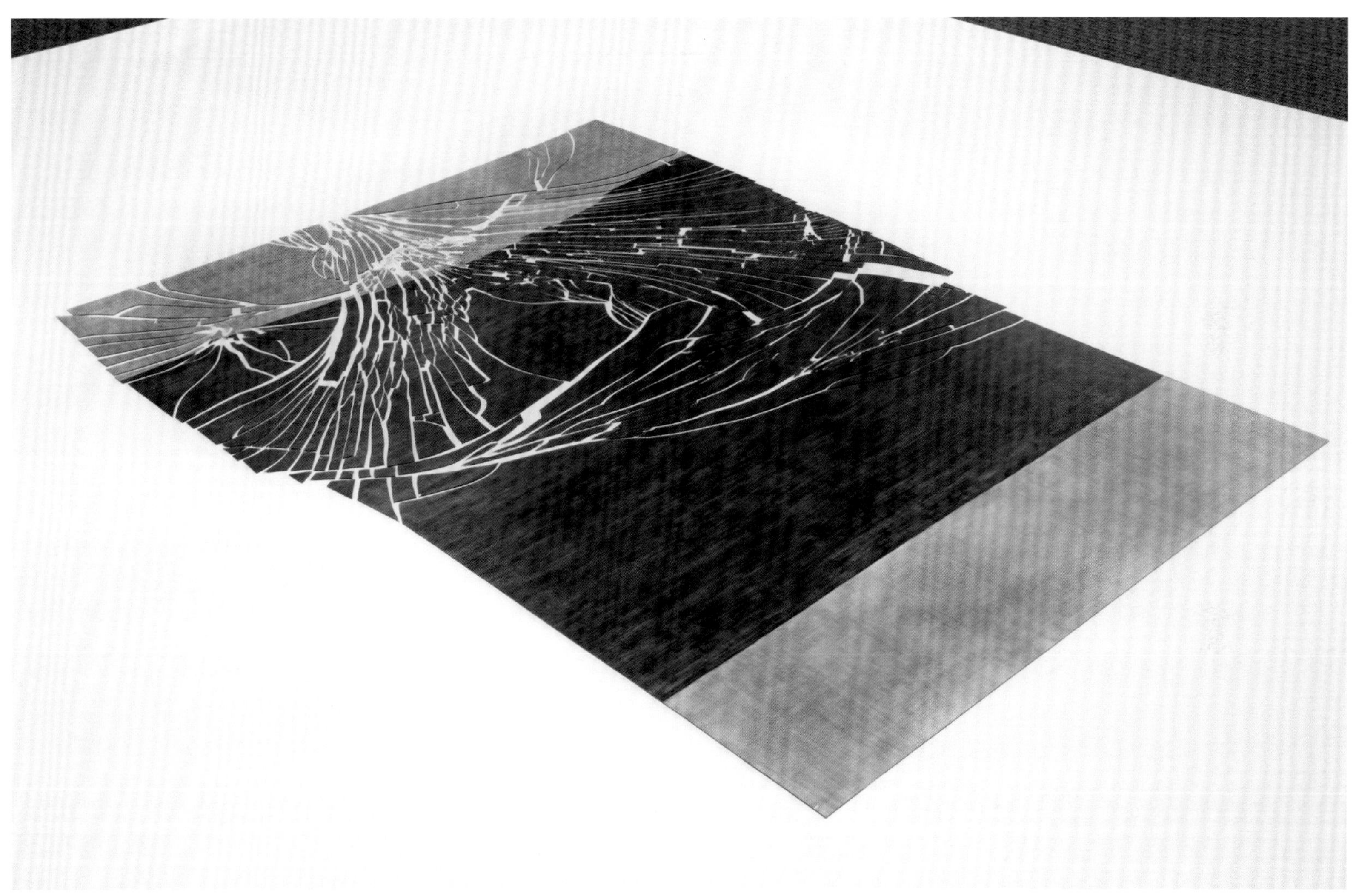

Perpetual Guest 2019/2022 Impossibility of Repair
(detail | détail), 2023
oil on glass and platform | huile sur vitre et plateforme
4 × 366 × 305 cm

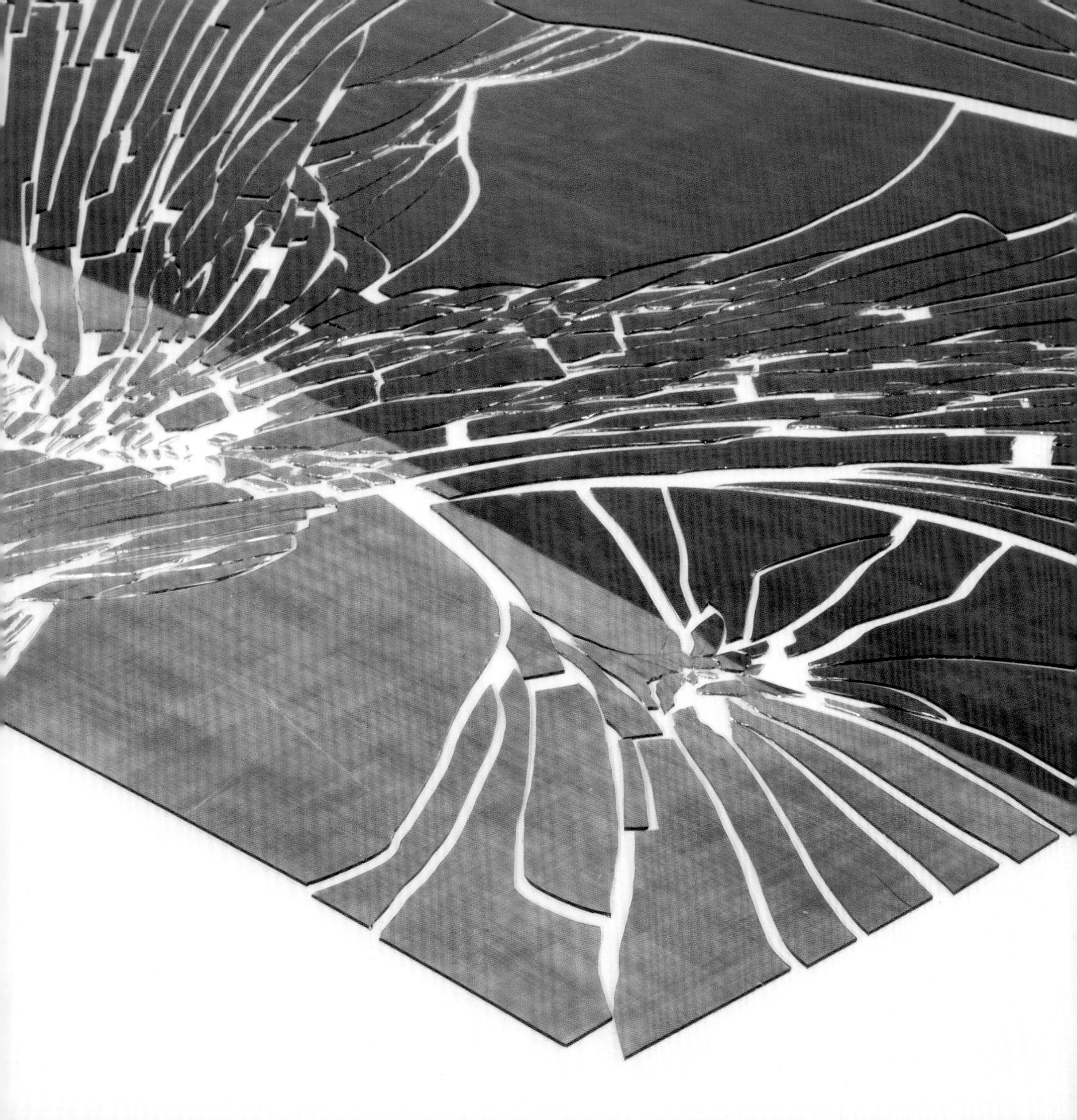

Perpetual Guest 2019/2022 Impossibility of Repair
(detail | détail), 2023
oil on glass and platform | huile sur vitre et plateforme
4 × 366 × 305 cm

Les peintures de Jinny Yu exigent que nous ralentissions et que nous prêtions attention, pour regarder d'une manière que nous avons oubliée. Pour nous permettre de voir au-delà du discours, dans une économie de l'attention qui ne demande qu'un engagement superficiel, de minuscules tranches de temps et des regards distraits. Les peintures de Yu ne crient pas, mais elles nous invitent à regarder, à écouter et à réfléchir de manière critique au-delà des apparences afin de remettre profondément en question et de réimaginer les structures.

À première vue, les œuvres sont faussement formalistes et semblent participer à une conversation moderniste sur la peinture qui, tout en revendiquant une histoire co-créée et transnationale de la forme qui entrelace habilement l'abstraction géométrique, le minimalisme, le Dansaekhwa et le Mono-ha, ne semble pas être explicitement politique. Les peintures de Yu ne sont pas, cependant, des formes pures, mais utilisent plutôt une recherche sur la forme comme porte d'entrée à une réflexion conceptuelle et politique. En peignant sur du coton qui se déplace au gré des courants d'air comme un souffle, sur du verre qui révèle le sol en dessous comme le désir et sur des panneaux d'aluminium qui apparaissent et disparaissent comme la lumière, Yu est une artiste qui explore les seuils de la peinture pour sonder les frontières que nous construisons en nous-mêmes, les façons dont nous organisons le monde et les cadres conceptuels que nous utilisons pour comprendre l'art, la vie et la politique.

> «Le monde brûle et je peins».
> – Jinny Yu

L'art abstrait peut-il être politique? L'art politique peut-il être abstrait? Quelle est la relation entre l'esthétique et la politique? Comment les peintures de Yu, qui explorent en profondeur des questions se répercutant dans le champ hermétique de la peinture *qua* peinture, parviennent-elles également à résonner au-delà de ce champ, produisant des vagues qui se propagent vers l'extérieur pour changer la façon dont nous nous percevons dans le monde, sur cette terre, et dans nos relations avec les autres? Comment Yu exploite-t-elle les possibilités de l'abstraction pour formuler de nouvelles façons d'être et de savoir?[1] Comment ces peintures offrent-elles aux spectateurs un langage affectif et formel pour imaginer le monde autrement (par d'autres moyens, ainsi qu'à travers d'autres formes de sagesse), dans un monde pluriversel au-delà des binarités et des positions incommensurables?[2]

Le tournant politique dans l'œuvre de Yu a commencé avec *Don't They Ever Stop Migrating?*, une installation picturale immersive créée en 2015 pour une exposition parallèle à *All the World's Futures*, la 56e Biennale de Venise commissariée par Okwui Enwezor. Dans le contexte de cette biennale, qui réfléchissait à des avenirs pour tous et pas seulement pour les privilégiés, l'œuvre de Yu était un acte de justice réparatrice qui attirait l'attention sur la crise de la migration désespérée en Méditerranée, tout en posant des questions difficiles sur la psychologie derrière la peur et le processus de l'altérisation (*Othering*).

L'œuvre consiste en une série de panneaux de coton souple installés pour créer une pièce, peints avec des coups de pinceau encrés qui se regroupent et se dispersent comme des murmurations. L'éparpillement des formes s'accompagne également d'un éparpillement de voix et de chuchotements étouffés et anxieux – un collage sonore que Yu a créé à partir du film *Les Oiseaux* d'Alfred Hitchcock (1963) et qui crée un environnement de panique : « D'où venez-vous? Qu'êtes-vous? Que se passe-t-il? Je pense que vous êtes à l'origine de tout ça! Vous effrayez les enfants… » chuchote un chœur de voix féminines. La peur oppressante évoquée par les voix n'est cependant pas continue et les silences qui s'y glissent permettent au spectateur de voir la beauté grandiose de la peinture de Yu, sa forme se modifiant avec les courants d'air et ouvrant des mondes au lieu de les fermer.

La tension entre l'ouverture mondiale du langage visuel de l'œuvre et la xénophobie de ses tonalités sonores invite le spectateur à reconsidérer la question de la migration à partir de perspectives et de positions multiples. Plutôt que de prendre parti et de produire des cloisonnements, l'œuvre crée généreusement un dialogue

1 David Getsy, « Reduction as Expansion: the Queer Capacities of Abstract Art ». Conférence publique, ICI Berlin, 1er février 2021.

2 Wayne Modest, « World Art Studies and the Ethnographic Museum », conférence, Université Carleton, 10 octobre, 2023; Tiffany Lethabo King, Jenell Navarro, et Andrea Smith, eds., *Otherwise worlds: Against settler colonialism and anti-Blackness* (Durham: Duke University Press, 2020).

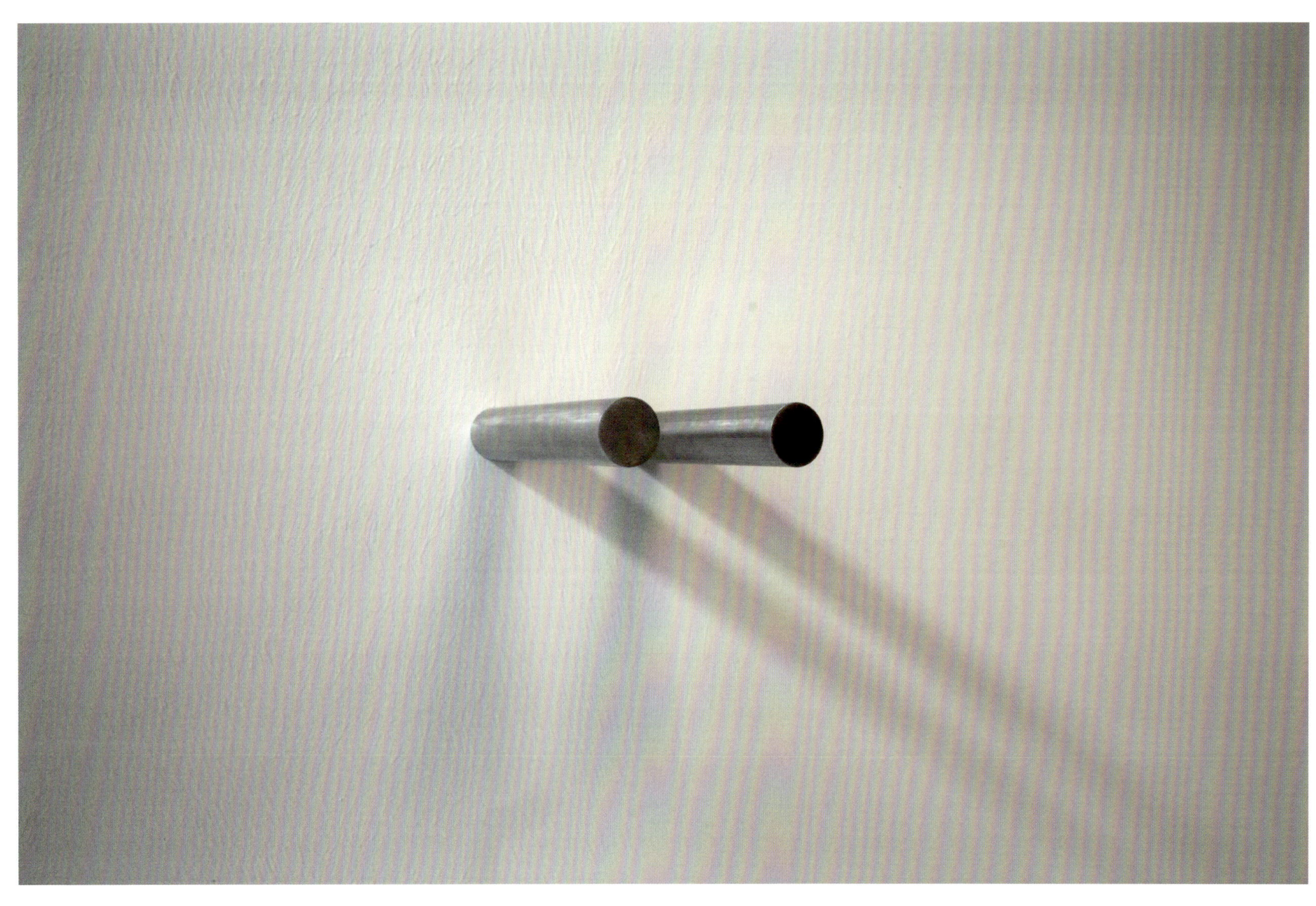

in a world without memory, 2018
aluminium
3 × 9 × 10 cm

sur ce que signifie la peur de l'inconnu, tout en offrant la possibilité de s'ouvrir à d'autres mondes, à d'autres positions et à d'autres modes de connaissance, un fait souligné par le médium de l'œuvre, l'encre sur coton. En faisant référence aux matériaux et aux méthodes de l'Asie de l'Est, l'œuvre remet en question la position par défaut et centrale occupée par les médiums occidentaux tels que l'huile ou l'acrylique sur toile, ce qui crée des mondes à travers d'autres matérialités.

Avec *Perpetual Guest* (2019), le propre lieu d'investigation de Yu s'est déplacé d'un contexte européen à un questionnement radical de sa relation avec la terre sur l'Île de la Tortue. Dans cette œuvre, le regard du spectateur pivote du haut dans *Don't They Ever Stop Migrating?* vers le bas, vers le sol; d'une réflexion sur les migrations à une réflexion sur les formes d'ancrage et d'atterrissage. L'œuvre consiste en une série de peintures réalisées à l'huile noire sur des panneaux de verre non trempé posés de manière précaire sur des pylônes en aluminium. Chaque panneau est une présence fantomatique, peinte en trois zones monochromes d'opacités différentes, flottant horizontalement à environ 10 cm du sol. En utilisant ce que l'artiste métis David Garneau caractérise comme une « stratégie [...] en survol – avoir plus d'espace, mais moins d'empreinte[3] », ces panneaux traitent de la politique de revendication d'un espace dans les institutions blanches par les artistes de couleur, mais résistent en même temps à la dissonance cognitive de l'implantation coloniale. En effet, lorsque l'œuvre a été exposée pour la première fois en 2019, à la Galerie UQO de Gatineau, au Québec, elle occupait une salle d'exposition dans laquelle le spectateur ne pouvait entrer sans marcher d'abord sur un texte au sol qui disait : « jinny yu : invitée perpétuelle sur ces terres non cédées de la nation algonquine anishinàbe ».

Mais qu'est-ce que cela signifie d'être un invité perpétuel, de non seulement résister aux privilèges présumés de l'appartenance, mais aussi de se libérer ainsi des responsabilités de la communauté ? Dans la série suivante, *Hôte* (2020), Yu a abordé cette question dans un cycle de dessins qu'elle a également transformé en livre d'artiste P. 54, 55. En superposant du graphite à base d'huile sur du papier dans des palimpsestes de temps, de gestes et de matériaux, Yu a créé 42 dessins qui ressemblent à des seuils. Ces travaux s'appuient sur les réflexions du philosophe français d'origine algérienne Jacques Derrida sur l'*hôte*, qui est un contronyme signifiant à la fois hôte et invité.[4] Consciente de sa propre position en tant qu'invitée

3 entretien #3 : *conversation between amy fung, david garneau and jinny yu on perpetual guest.* (Gatineau : Galerie de l'UQO, 2019), p. 20.

4 Jacques Derrida et Anne Dufourmantelle, *Of Hospitality.* (Stanford: Stanford University Press, 2000).

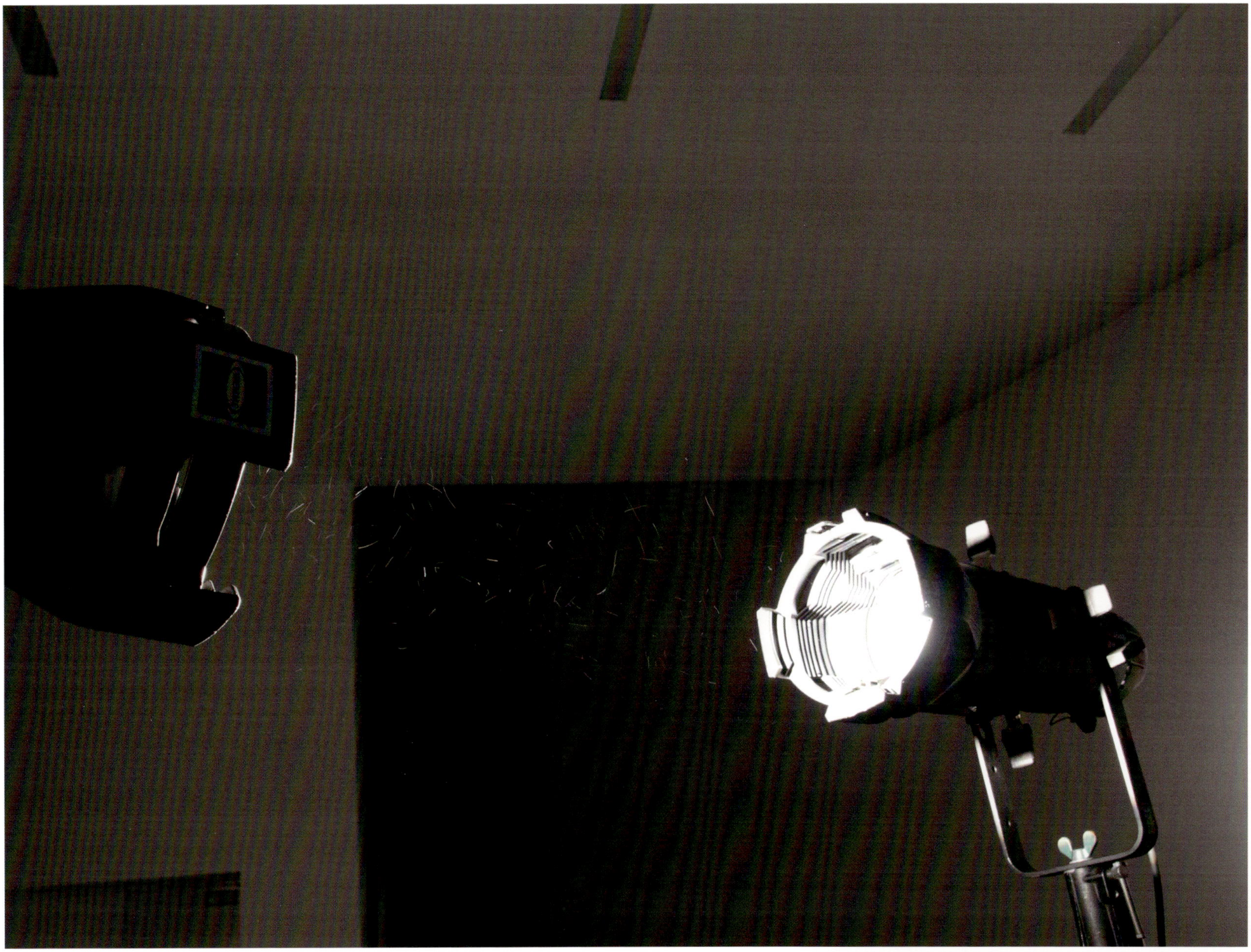

A study to reveal impurity, 2016
lights, electricity, air | lumière, électricité, air

Installation view | vue d'installation,
Individuating
July 29, 2016 | 29 juillet 2016
Kunstverein am Rosa-Luxemburg-Platz, Berlin

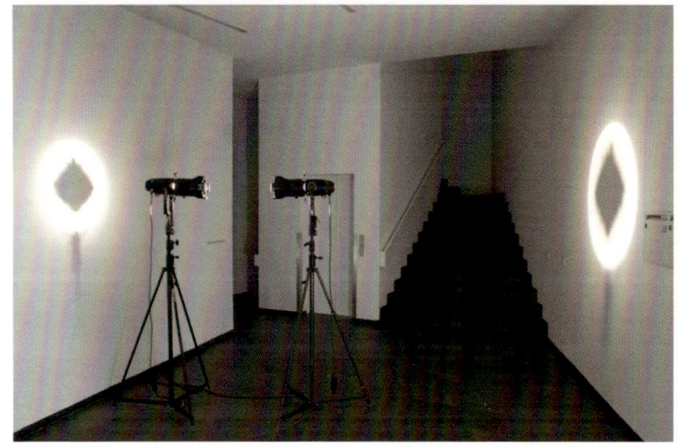

bienvenue d'un invité indésirable sur les terres autochtones, Yu remet néanmoins en question le sentiment problématique de responsabilité limitée que les invités peuvent percevoir pour eux-mêmes, recherchant des modes d'appartenance à travers la responsabilité plutôt que la possession. Elle demande : «Un invité peut-il être un hôte? Un hôte peut-il être un invité?» La série commence par des délimitations claires entre le noir et le blanc, qui représentent l'hôte et l'invité, mais au fur et à mesure qu'elle progresse, les lignes deviennent de plus en plus imbriquées, jusqu'à se transformer en configurations de gris sur gris. Comme l'écrit l'anthropologue Tim Ingold : «Les âmes, pourrions-nous dire, sont responsables les unes des autres, une condition qui implique à la fois réactivité et responsabilité.[5]»

Yu approfondit le contronyme d'*Hôte* en abordant la question de la relationalité dans la série *Inextricably Ours* (2021), et ce, par le biais de la forme visuelle. Dans cette série, elle peint des formes géométriques qui sont des figures *multistables*, ou *kippbilder*. L'exemple classique de telles figures est le canard/lapin, qui est évoqué par Ernst Gombrich dans *L'Art et l'illusion*, dont le bec se transforme en longues oreilles grâce à un changement dans la perception du spectateur. Ces formes, qui oscillent optiquement entre la figure et le fond, permettent la coexistence d'affirmations contradictoires «sans pour autant éliminer les différences entre des récits contradictoires ou établir une synthèse supérieure[6]». C'est ici que Yu commence à imaginer la figure se transformant en fond et de nouveau en figure, donnant une forme visuelle aux réflexions de Derrida sur l'*hôte* en tant que relation d'hospitalité, d'attention et de respect mutuel. Dans cette formulation, l'invité est aussi responsable envers l'hôte que l'hôte est responsable envers l'invité, chacun d'entre nous étant un invité de passage dans ce monde terrestre.

Le travail consistant à atteindre ce niveau de relationnalité, à négocier ce que Wanda Nanibush et Georgiana Uhlyarik décrivent comme une «relation de traité» décolonisatrice à travers des passés brisés et des histoires difficiles, est ardu et continu.[7] En 2020, lors de l'exposition de *Perpetual Guest*, un visiteur de la galerie a marché sur l'œuvre, la brisant en éclats. Yu a fait rapatrier les pièces à son atelier où, durant son isolement pandémique, elle les a minutieusement assemblées

5 Tim Ingold, « One World Anthropology », HAU Journal of Ethnographic Theory 9 no. 1 (2018): 160.

6 Christoph Holzhey dir., *Multistable Figures: On the Critical Potential of Ir/Reversible Aspect-Seeing* (Vienna: Turia + Kant, 2014), p. 7.

7 Wanda Nanibush et Georgiana Uhlyarik, eds., *Moving the Museum: Indigenous + Canadian Art at the AGO*. (Fredericton: Goose Lane Editions; Toronto: Art Gallery of Ontario, 2023); Wanda Nanibush et Georgiana Uhlyarik, dans *Worlding the Global : The Arts in the Age of Decolonization*, dir. Birgit Hopfener et Ming Tiampo (Berlin: ICI Berlin Press, à paraître en 2024).

pour créer une nouvelle œuvre, *Perpetual Guest 2019/2022 Impossibility of Repair* (2023). Assemblage sans colle, l'œuvre est désormais marquée par sa temporalité délibérée et sa relation avec le sol, les fissures fonctionnant désormais comme des sites d'ouverture, de friction et de reconfiguration constante, qui fracturent la distance précédemment assurée par l'intégralité de *Perpetual Guest*. Chacun des fragments est une entité propre, mais fonctionne en relation intime avec des espaces vierges et d'autres fragments pour créer des paysages et des histoires qui sont à la fois brisés, multiples et continuellement réimaginés.[8]

Reflétant la façon dont elle a permis au monde d'entrer par les fissures de *Perpetual Guest*, la pratique de Yu s'ouvre à une modalité activiste qui est implicite dans sa peinture. La plus importante de ses activités en matière de pratique collaborative, de commissariat discursif, de pédagogie radicale et d'organisation communautaire est peut-être le *Canadian BIPOC Artists Rolodex* (CBIPOCAR), un projet d'humanités numériques qu'elle a lancé avec Celina Jeffery et moi-même, en dialogue avec la curatrice de données Felicity Tayler.

CBIPOCAR est une base de données revisitée qui rend visibles les artistes BIPOC (noirs, autochtones, personnes de couleur) au Canada et qui est conçue pour accroître la recherche, l'enseignement et les expositions sur les artistes BIPOC. En tant que Rolodex, un outil de gestion de contacts, le projet vise également à établir des relations et est conçu pour connecter les artistes BIPOC entre eux, à la fois numériquement et par le biais d'activités discursives planifiées. Yu a initialement conçu CBIPOCAR en réponse à l'affirmation selon laquelle les artistes BIPOC sont difficiles à intégrer dans un programme d'enseignement des arts visuels parce qu'ils sont difficiles à trouver. Dans les contextes montants des mouvements Black Lives Matter, Idle No More et Stop Asian Hate, le projet est cependant devenu une stratégie décoloniale importante pour aborder le fait que les artistes BIPOC ont peu de représentation institutionnelle, sont moins exposés, sont moins enseignés en classe et, plus important encore, sont discursivement moins visibles dans les histoires et les récits de l'art canadien.

En plus des projets empiriques de collecte de données et de narration, CBIPOCAR est aussi nécessairement engagé dans des études critiques de données, cherchant à décoloniser les hypothèses faites par la science des données sur l'identité, le médium, et même la nature et les définitions de l'art. Qui est inclus

8 Des parties de cette analyse sont basées sur l'introduction de Birgit Hopfener et Ming Tiampo, *Worlding the Global : The Arts in the Age of Decolonization* (Berlin : ICI Berlin Press, à paraître en 2024).

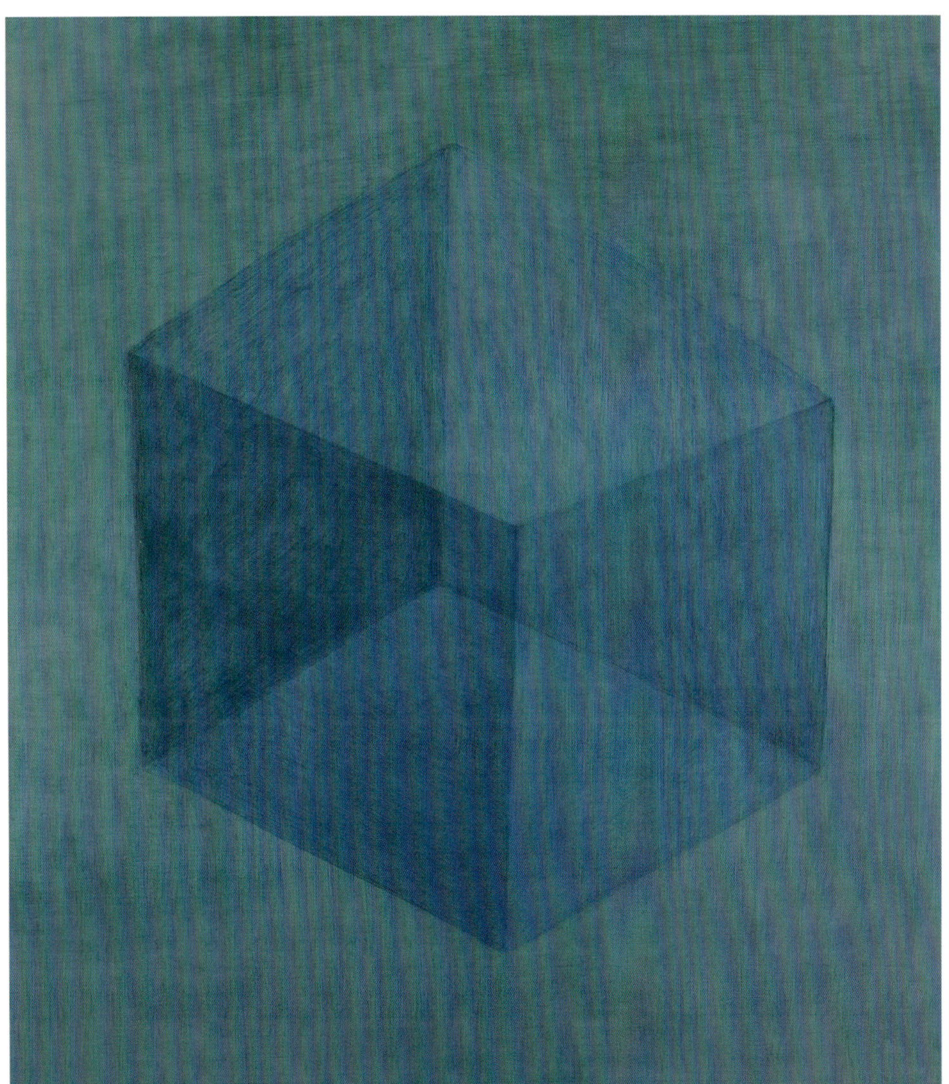

Inextricably Ours 21-01, 2022
oil on aluminium | huile sur aluminium
100 × 92 cm

dans un groupe identitaire? Qui décide? Quelle nomenclature devrions-nous utiliser? Qui devrait avoir accès à ces informations? Quels médiums devraient être indexés? Comment définir l'art et comment l'appeler? Réunissant un comité consultatif de 19 membres composé d'artistes, de commissaires et d'universitaires BIPOC, le projet s'attaque ainsi aux similitudes, aux différences et aux interconnexions inhérentes à la manière dont ces différents groupes œuvrant solidairement imaginent des champs catégoriels, tout en reconnaissant que de telles catégories ne sont jamais neutres. À l'instar de la reconfiguration de *Perpetual Guest* à partir de ses fragments, ces discussions remettent en question les binarismes cloisonnés et réimaginent de possibles relations, formes, paysages, histoires et langages.

En procédant autrement, la pratique multiforme de Yu ouvre des mondes par le biais de recherches qui proposent des manières pluriverselles de connaître et de voir, des *figures multistables* qui maintiennent ensemble des réalités multiples et parfois conflictuelles : *À la fois*.

À la fois matière et image
À la fois concrétude et représentation
À la fois figure et fond
À la fois un et plusieurs
À la fois figuratif et abstrait
À la fois objectif et non objectif
À la fois hôte et invité
À la fois ici et ailleurs
À la fois peinture et activisme
À la fois poétique et politique
À la fois données et histoires
À la fois matière et lumière
À la fois clarté et opacité
À la fois connu et inconnu
À la fois voir et lire
À la fois ressentir et savoir
À la fois individuel et collectif
À la fois invité et hôte
À la fois colonisateur et colonisé
À la fois héritages et avenirs
À la fois Soi, Autre et autrement ■

↓ *Perpetual Guest 2019/2022 Impossibility of Repair* (detail | détail), 2023
oil on glass and platform | huile sur vitre et plateforme
4 × 366 × 305 cm

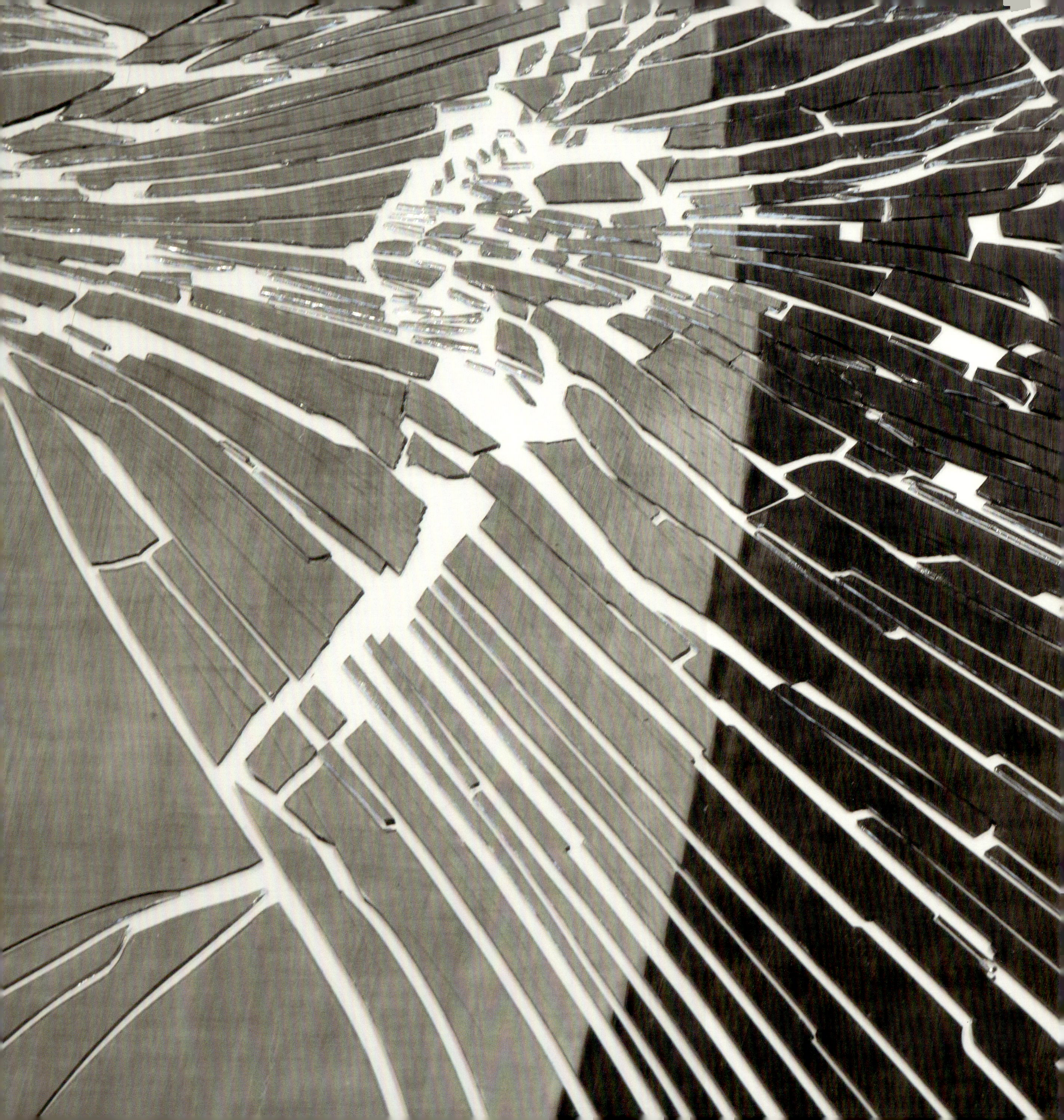

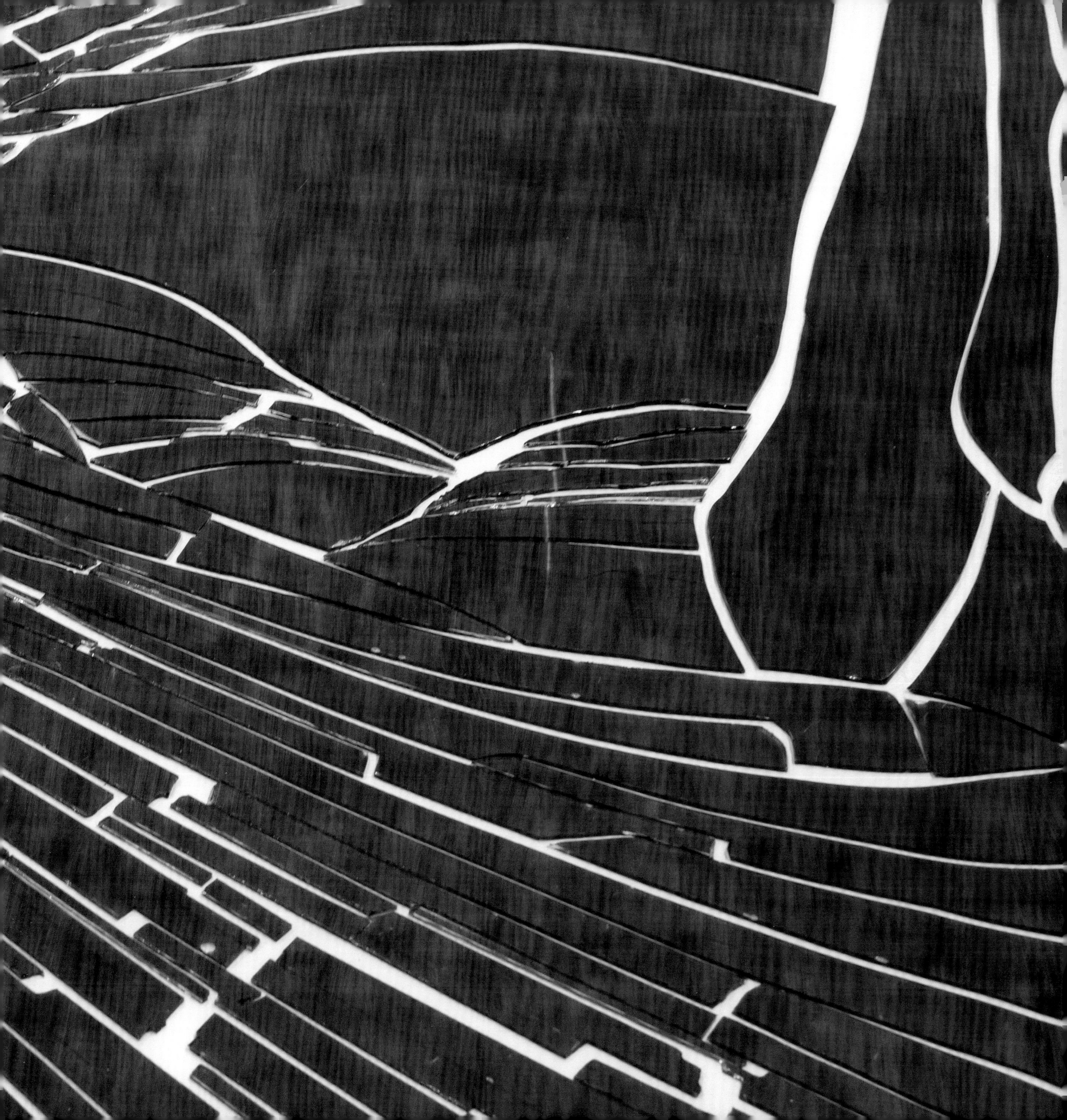

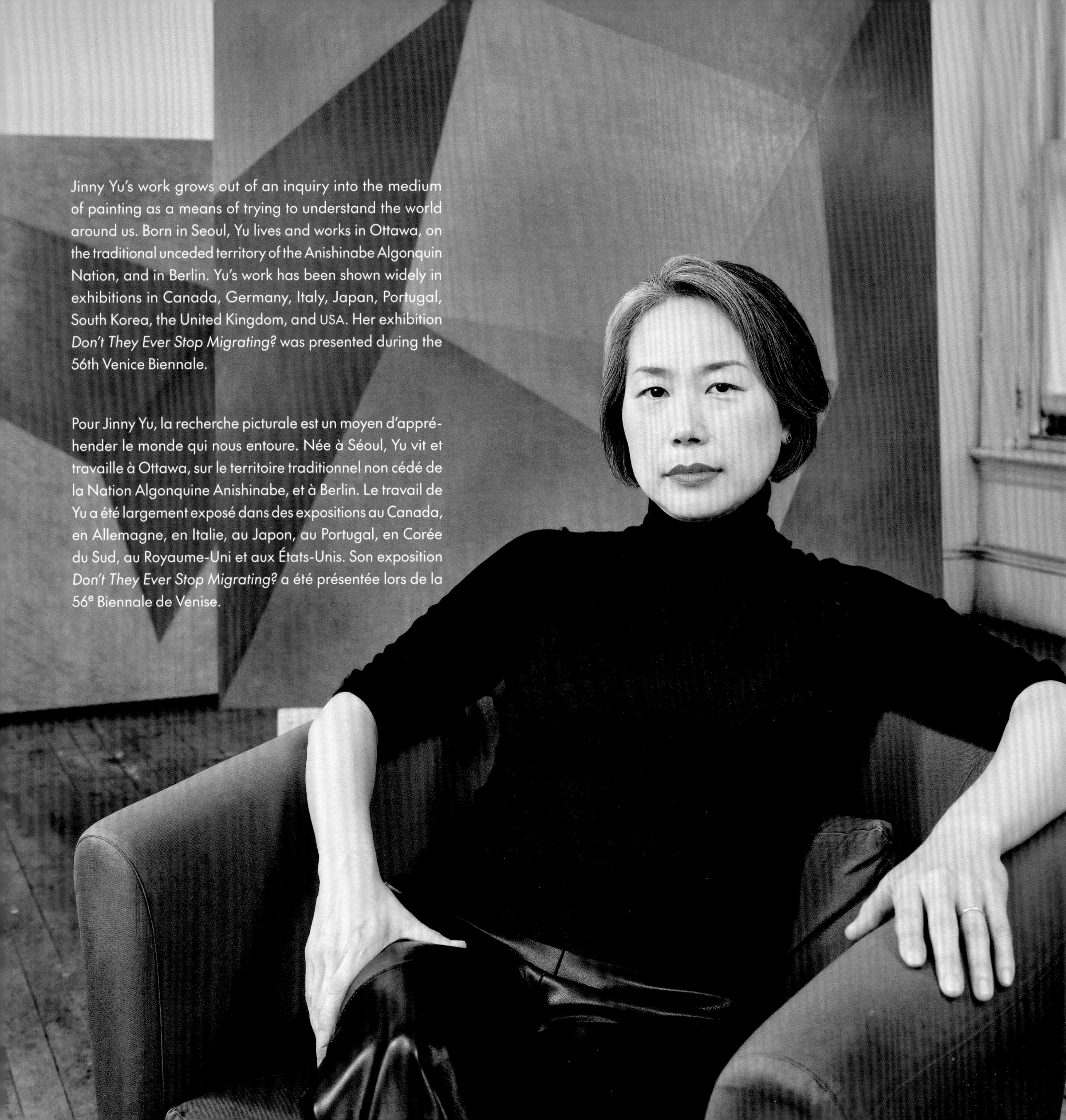

Jinny Yu's work grows out of an inquiry into the medium of painting as a means of trying to understand the world around us. Born in Seoul, Yu lives and works in Ottawa, on the traditional unceded territory of the Anishinabe Algonquin Nation, and in Berlin. Yu's work has been shown widely in exhibitions in Canada, Germany, Italy, Japan, Portugal, South Korea, the United Kingdom, and USA. Her exhibition *Don't They Ever Stop Migrating?* was presented during the 56th Venice Biennale.

Pour Jinny Yu, la recherche picturale est un moyen d'appréhender le monde qui nous entoure. Née à Séoul, Yu vit et travaille à Ottawa, sur le territoire traditionnel non cédé de la Nation Algonquine Anishinabe, et à Berlin. Le travail de Yu a été largement exposé dans des expositions au Canada, en Allemagne, en Italie, au Japon, au Portugal, en Corée du Sud, au Royaume-Uni et aux États-Unis. Son exposition *Don't They Ever Stop Migrating?* a été présentée lors de la 56e Biennale de Venise.

Solo Exhibitions | Expositions individuelles

2020 *Hôte*, Art Mûr Montréal, Canada
2019 *Perpetual Guest*, Galerie UQO, Gatineau, Canada
2018 *that the problem is not a problem for me is a part of the problem*, Art Mûr Berlin, Germany
2018 *Not Even Silence Gets Us Out of the Circle*, Contemporary Art Institute, Daegu, South Korea
2015–16 *Don't They Ever Stop Migrating?*, Nuova Icona, 56th Venice Biennale, Venice, Italy; The Rooms, St. John's, Canada
2013 *I am Painting*, Galerie du Nouvel-Ontario, Sudbury, Canada
2013 *Black Matter*, Sookmyung Women's University Museum, Seoul, Korea
2012 *Non-Painting Painting*, Kunst Doc Art Gallery, Seoul, Korea

Two-Person Exhibitions | Expositions en duo

2023 *Marina Roy, Jinny Yu & The Painted Object*, Royal Canadian Academy of Arts | Académie royale des arts du Canada, Ottawa, Canada
2014 *Just That: Jinny Yu and Takaya Fujii*, Produzentengalerie plan.d., Düsseldorf, Germany
2011–13 *Cadenza*, Confederation Centre Art Gallery | Musée d'art du Centre de la Confédération, Charlottetown; St. Mary's University Art Gallery, Halifax; McMaster Museum of Art, Hamilton; Stewart Hall Art Gallery | Galerie d'art Stewart Hall, Montréal, Canada

Group Exhibitions | Expositions de groupes

2023 *Aterritorial*, Joshua Treenial, BoxoPROJECTS, Joshua Tree, USA
2023 *International Garden Festival*, Reford Gardens | Jardins de Métis, Grand-Métis, Canada
2020 *RELATIONS: Diaspora and Painting*, PHI Foundation for Contemporary Art | Fondation PHI pour l'art contemporain, Montréal; Esker Foundation, Calgary, Canada
2019 *Contemporary artists at play: Flirting with Codes*, Tricks and Subterfuge, Montréal Museum of Fine Arts | Musée des beaux-arts de Montréal, Canada
2016 *Yonder*, Koffler Centre of the Arts, Toronto, Canada
2016 *Individuating*, Kunstverein am Rosa-Luxemburg-Platz, Berlin, Germany
2016 *Style of the Between*, 10th Taehwa Eco-River Art Festival 16, Ulsan City, Korea
2015 *The Conceptual Impulse Today, Part 2*, Busche Kunst, Berlin, Germany

Artist Residencies | Résidences d'artiste

2022 La Napoule Art Foundation Canadian Artist Residency | Résidence pour Artistes Canadiens, France
2022 BoxoPROJECTS Contemporary Art at the New Frontier, Joshua Tree, California, USA
2018 Klondike Institute of Art and Culture, Dawson City, Yukon, Canada
2012 Nanji Art Studio, Seoul Museum of Art, Seoul, Korea
2010–11 International Studio & Curatorial Program, Brooklyn, New York, USA

Bibliography | Bibliographie

Cheetham, Mark A. and | et Penny Cousineau-Levine. *Jinny Yu: To Activate Space*. Montréal: Éditions Art Mûr; Ottawa: Ottawa Art Gallery, 2014.

Fabo, Andy and | et Dermot Wilson. *New Century Abstracts*. Peterborough: Peterborough Art Gallery, 2014.

Foscari, Antonio, Emily Falvey and | et Édith-Anne Pageot. *Jinny Yu*. Ottawa: University of Ottawa Press; Montréal: Éditions Art Mûr, 2008.

Fung, Amy, David Garneau and | et Jinny Yu. *Entretiens #3: Conversation between Amy Fung, David Garneau and Jinny Yu on Perpetual Guest*. Gatineau: Galerie UQO; Montréal: Anteism Books, 2019.

Halkes, Petra. "Jinny Yu." *In Construction Work*. Ottawa: Carleton University Art Gallery, 2010.

Shaughnessy, Jonathan. "Jinny Yu – Perpetual Guest." In | dans *RELATIONS: Diaspora and Painting | la diaspora et la peinture*, edited by | sous la direction de Cheryl Sim. Munich: Hirmer Publishers, 2020, 196-203.

Public Collections | Collections publiques

Agnes Etherington Art Centre
Art Gallery of Ontario | Musée des beaux-arts de l'Ontario, Edward P. Taylor Library & Archives
Canada Council Art Bank | Banque d'art du Conseil des arts du Canada
City of | Ville d'Ottawa
Confederation Centre Art Gallery | Musée d'art du Centre de la Confédération
Global Affairs Canada | Affaires mondiales Canada
Montreal Museum of Fine Arts | Musée des beaux-arts de Montréal
Musée national des beaux-arts du Québec
Ottawa Art Gallery | Galerie d'art d'Ottawa

Patrick Flores is Professor of Art Studies at the Department of Art Studies at the University of the Philippines and concurrently Deputy Director at National Gallery Singapore. He was a Visiting Fellow at the National Gallery of Art in Washington, D.C. in 1999. He was a Guest Scholar of the Getty Research Institute in Los Angeles in 2014. He was the Artistic Director of Singapore Biennale 2019 and Curator (Convener of Forums) of the Taiwan Pavilion at the Venice Biennale in 2022.

Ming Tiampo is Professor of Art History, and co-director of the Centre for Transnational Cultural Analysis at Carleton University. Tiampo's major projects include *Gutai: Decentering Modernism* (University of Chicago Press, 2011); *Gutai: Splendid Playground*, co-curated at the Guggenheim Museum in New York (2013); and *Jin-me Yoon* (Art Canada Institute, 2022). Her current book *Transversal Modernism/s: The Slade School of Fine Art*, reimagines transcultural intersections through global microhistory. Tiampo is co-principal investigator of *Worlding Public Cultures*.

Georgiana Uhlyarik is Fredrik S. Eaton Curator, Canadian Art, and co-lead of the Indigenous + Canadian Art Department at the Art Gallery of Ontario, Toronto, Canada. She works collaboratively with artists and curators from across the Americas and Europe. Projects include: *Moving the Museum: Indigenous + Canadian Art at the AGO*; *Magnetic North: Imagining Canada in Painting 1910-1940* (Schirn Kunsthalle Frankfurt); *Tunirrusiangit: Kenojuak Ashevak and Tim Pitsiulak*, *Rita Letendre: Fire & Light*; *Georgia O'Keeffe* (Tate Modern), and *Florine Stettheimer: Painting Poetry* (Jewish Museum, NY). Uhlyarik is adjunct faculty in Art, York University and University of Toronto.

Director of the Guido Molinari Foundation since 2023, **Marie-Eve Beaupré** has collaborated with various institutions over the past twenty years. She was curator of the collection at the Musée d'art contemporain de Montréal (2016-2023) and curator of Contemporary Quebec and Canadian Art at the Montreal Museum of Fine Arts (2014-2016). She also collaborated with the Musée national des beaux-arts du Québec (2010-2014) and the Galerie de l'UQAM (2004-2012) on exhibition and research projects. As an art historian and field practitioner, she has been involved in several inventories, including the studios of Edmund Alleyn, Sylvia Safdie, John Heward, Betty Goodwin and Guido Molinari.

Patrick Flores est professeur en Études des arts au département en Études des arts à l'Université des Philippines et, parallèlement, directeur adjoint de la Galerie nationale de Singapour. Il a été chercheur invité à la Galerie nationale d'art à Washington, D.C. en 1999 et à l'Institut de Recherche Getty à Los Angeles en 2014. Il a été directeur artistique de la Biennale de Singapour 2019 et commissaire (organisateur de forums) du pavillon de Taïwan à la Biennale de Venise en 2022.

Ming Tiampo est professeure d'histoire de l'art et codirectrice du Centre d'analyse culturelle transnationale de l'Université de Carleton. Les principaux projets de Tiampo comprennent *Gutai: Decentering Modernism* (Presses de l'Université de Chicago, 2011), *Gutai : Splendid Playground* en collaboration avec le Musée Guggenheim à New York (2013), et *Jin-me Yoon* (Institut de l'art canadien, 2022). Son récent livre, *Transversal Modernism/s: The Slade School of Fine Art*, réimagine les intersections transculturelles par le biais de la microhistoire mondiale. Tiampo est co-chercheuse principale de Worlding Public Cultures.

Georgiana Uhlyarik est conservatrice Fredrik S. Eaton pour l'art canadien et codirectrice du département de l'art autochtone et canadien au Musée des beaux-arts de l'Ontario, à Toronto. Elle travaille en collaboration avec des artistes et commissaires de l'Amérique et de l'Europe. Ses projets incluent : *Moving the Museum: Indigenous + Canadian Art at the AGO*; *Magnetic North: Imagining Canada in Painting 1910-1940* (Schirn Kunsthalle Frankfurt); *Tunirrusiangit: Kenojuak Ashevak and Tim Pitsiulak*; *Rita Letendre: Fire & Light*; *Georgia O'Keeffe* (Tate Modern); *Florine Stettheimer: Painting Poetry* (Musée Juif, NY). Uhlyarik est professeure adjointe en Arts à l'Université York et à l'Université de Toronto.

Directrice de la Fondation Guido Molinari depuis 2023, **Marie-Eve Beaupré** a collaboré avec diverses institutions au cours des vingt dernières années. Elle fut conservatrice de la collection au Musée d'art contemporain de Montréal (2016-2023) et conservatrice de l'art contemporain québécois et canadien au Musée des beaux-arts de Montréal (2014-2016). Elle a également collaboré avec le Musée national des beaux-arts du Québec (2010-2014) et la Galerie de l'UQAM (2004-2012) pour des projets d'exposition et de recherche. Historienne de l'art et praticienne de terrain, elle a réalisé plusieurs inventaires, dont celui des ateliers d'Edmund Alleyn, Sylvia Safdie, John Heward, Betty Goodwin et Guido Molinari.

Published in conjunction with the exhibition *JINNY YU: AT ONCE*, curated by Georgiana Uhlyarik at the Art Gallery of Ontario.
The itinerary of the exhibition is as follows:
Art Gallery of Ontario, Toronto: June 22, 2024 – January 5, 2025
Guido Molinari Foundation, Montréal: June 5 – August 24, 2025
(curated by Art/Around in collaboration with Georgiana Uhlyarik).

Publication director: Studio Jinny Yu.
Cover and page design: bureau60a.
Translation of the preface into English: Bernard Schütze.
Copy editor: Nancy Wallace.
Translation of the essays into French: Béatrice Larochelle.
Photography: Aylin Abbasi (20, 32, 33, 40, 41);
Francesco Allegretto (86, 89, 95 bottom, 97); Tom Bartlett (99);
Maryn Devine (72, 73, 75, 76, 78); Darrell Edwards (90-2, 95 top);
Steve Farmer (58, 61, 62, 67, 69, 81); Neeko Paluzzi (102-4, 114, 115);
Adrienne Row - Smith (116); John Tamblyn (83);
Rémi Thériault (27, 29, 31, 34-39, 44, 112);
Richard-Max Tremblay (24, 48, 56, 57, 64, 74); Eric Tschernow (107);
Sean Weaver (14, 17-9, 42, 43) ©AGO;
Andrew Wright (22, 46, 54, 55); Jinny Yu (2-5, 10, 11, 109).
Cover image: Jinny Yu, *Inextricably Ours 22-05*, 2022, oil on aluminum, 152 × 140 cm.
Private collection. Photo: Rémi Thériault.
All works courtesy of the artist unless otherwise noted.
Printed in Canada by Friesens.
10 9 8 7 6 5 4 3 2 1

Library and Archives Canada Cataloguing in Publication

Title: Jinny Yu : at once = à la fois.
Other titles: At once | À la fois | Jinny Yu (2024) | Jinny Yu (2024). French
Names: Yu, Jinny, 1976- Paintings. Selections.
Description: Authors : Marie-Eve Beaupré, Georgiana Uhlyarik, Patrick Flores, Ming Tiampo. | Catalogue of an exhibition organized by the Art Gallery of Ontario. | Includes bibliographical references. | Text in English and French.
Identifiers: Canadiana 20240342399E | ISBN 9781773104270 (hardcover)
Subjects: LCSH: Yu, Jinny, 1976-—Exhibitions. | LCGFT: Exhibition catalogs.
Classification: LCC ND249.Y82 A4 2024 | DDC 759.11—dc23

The artist and the publisher wish to acknowledge the contributions of the following individuals and institutions: Glen Bloom and Deborah Duffy, University of Ottawa, Art Gallery of Ontario, Guido Molinari Foundation, Government of Canada, Canada Council for the Arts, and Government of New Brunswick.

Goose Lane Editions is located on the unceded territory of the Wəlastəkwiyik whose ancestors along with the Mi'kmaq and Peskotomuhkati Nations signed Peace and Friendship Treaties with the British Crown in the 1700s.

Goose Lane Editions
500 Beaverbrook Court, Suite 330
Fredericton, New Brunswick
CANADA E3B 5X4
gooselane.com

Publie à l'occasion de l'exposition *JINNY YU: AT ONCE*, commissarié par Georgiana Uhlyarik au Musée des beaux-arts de l'Ontario.
L'itinéraire de l'exposition est le suivant :
Musée des beaux-arts de l'Ontario, Toronto : 22 juin 2024 – 5 janvier 2025
Fondation Guido Molinari, Montréal : 5 juin – 24 août 2025
(commissarié par Art/Around en collaboration avec Georgiana Uhlyarik).

Direction de la publication : Studio Jinny Yu
Conception de la couverture et design graphique : bureau60a
Traduction des essais vers français : Béatrice Larochelle
Révision de la version française : Amélie Hamel et Béatrice Larochelle
Traduction de la préface vers anglais : Bernard Schütze
Crédits photographiques : Aylin Abbasi (20, 32, 33, 40, 41);
Francesco Allegretto (86, 89, 95 bas, 97); Tom Bartlett (99);
Maryn Devine (72, 73, 75, 76, 78); Darrell Edwards (90-2, 95 haut);
Steve Farmer (58, 61, 62, 67, 69, 81); Neeko Paluzzi (102-4, 114, 115);
Adrienne Row - Smith (116); John Tamblyn (83);
Rémi Thériault (27, 29, 31, 34-39, 44, 112);
Richard-Max Tremblay (24, 48, 56, 57, 64, 74); Eric Tschernow (107);
Sean Weaver (14, 17-9, 42, 43) ©AGO;
Andrew Wright (22, 46, 54, 55); Jinny Yu (2-5, 10, 11, 109)
Photo de la couverture : Jinny Yu, *Inextricably Ours 22-05*, 2022, huile sur aluminium, 152 × 140 cm. Collection privée. Photo : Rémi Thériault.
Toutes les œuvres sont gracieusement fournies par l'artiste, sauf indication contraire.
Imprimé au Canada par Friesens.
10 9 8 7 6 5 4 3 2 1

Catalogage avant publication de Bibliothèque et Archives Canada

Titre : Jinny Yu: at once = à la fois.
Autres titres : At once | À la fois | Jinny Yu (2024) | Jinny Yu (2024). Français
Noms : Yu, Jinny, 1976- Peintures. Extraits.
Description: Auteurs : Marie-Eve Beaupré, Georgiana Uhlyarik, Patrick Flores, Ming Tiampo. | Catalogue d'une exposition organisée par le Musée des beaux-arts de l'Ontario. | Comprend des références bibliographiques. | Texte en anglais et en français.
Identifiants : Canadiana 20240342399F | ISBN 9781773104270 (couverture rigide)
Vedettes-matière : RVM : Yu, Jinny, 1976-—Expositions. | RVMGF : Catalogues d'exposition.
Classification : LCC ND249.Y82 A4 2024 | CDD 759.11—dc23

L'artiste et Goose Lane Editions reconnaîssent le généreux soutien des individus et des institutions suivantes : Glen Bloom et Deborah Duffy, l'Université d'Ottawa, le Musée des beaux-arts de l'Ontario, la Fondation Guido Molinari, le gouvernement du Canada, le Conseil des arts du Canada et le gouvernement du Nouveau-Brunswick.

Goose Lane Editions est situé sur le territoire non cédé des Wəlastəkwiyik, dont les ancêtres, ainsi que les nations des Mi'kmaq et des Peskotomuhkati, ont signé des traités de paix et d'amitié avec la Couronne britannique dans les années 1700.

Goose Lane Editions
500, cour Beaverbrook, bureau 330
Fredericton (Nouveau-Brunswick)
CANADA E3B 5X4
gooselane.com